W9-BYL-100

Mindful
Parenting

Mindful Parenting

SIMPLE and **POWERFUL SOLUTIONS** for **RAISING CREATIVE, ENGAGED, HAPPY KIDS** in Today's Hectic World

Kristen Race, Ph.D.

St. Martin's Griffin
New York

This book is dedicated to Macy & Charlie
I am forever grateful for your hugs, your kisses, and your smiling faces.
Thank you for always reminding of the
exquisiteness of the present moment.

MINDFUL PARENTING. Copyright © 2013 by Kristen Race, Ph.D. All rights reserved. Printed in the United States of America. For information, address St. Martin's Press, 175 Fifth Avenue, New York, N.Y. 10010.

Forty Developmental Assets® for Middle Childhood (Ages 8–12), pages 216–20, are reprinted with permission from Search Institute, Minneapolis, Minnesota. For more information, please visit www.search-institute.org.

www.stmartins.com

Library of Congress Cataloging-in-Publication Data

Race, Kristen.
     Mindful parenting : simple and powerful solutions for raising creative, engaged, happy kids in today's hectic world / Kristen Race, Ph.D.—First edition.
          pp. cm.
     Includes index.
     ISBN 978-1-250-02031-4 (trade paperback)
     ISBN 978-1-250-02032-1 (e-book)
  1. Parenting. 2. Meditation—Therapeutic use. 3. Stress management.
I. Title.
     HQ755.8.R29 2013
     306.874—dc23   2013020553

St. Martin's Griffin books may be purchased for educational, business, or promotional use. For information on bulk purchases, please contact Macmillan Corporate and Premium Sales Department at 1-800-221-7945, extension 5442, or write specialmarkets@macmillan.com.

First Edition: January 2014

10 9 8 7 6 5 4 3 2 1

CONTENTS

PART I

Today's Family

When Everything You Know About Parenting Goes Out the Window

Remember when life's biggest stress was deciding where to meet friends for dinner or what to wear on Friday night? Remember when having fun was foremost on your agenda? If you're anything like me, things have changed.

For me the change came at around the age of twenty-eight. After deciding it was time to do more with my life than be the eternal ski bum, I got married, went to graduate school, had a beautiful baby girl, and then landed the perfect job in Denver. I was hired as the director of counseling services by a top-notch independent school that ran pre-K through twelfth grade. It was demanding, particularly as I tried to balance a full-time job with being a new mom and finishing my doctorate.

Things got even more interesting when I found out baby number two was on the way. With the clock running out, the pressure was on for me to finish my dissertation (when I wasn't at work) while still spending time with my family. And I had only six months before my second child was born. Call it some strong nesting instinct, but I also decided that it was the perfect time to remodel my house!

Believing I could handle anything if I set my mind to it, I managed to defend my dissertation and graduate one month before my son arrived. The house was finished and looked beautiful; my job was demanding but rewarding; my daughter loved her child care center; and I was still happily married.

As many of you know, it is amazing what your mind and body can do when you're under the gun. It was stress that drove me to accomplish what I did: to be the perfect mom, to have the perfect career, and to create the "perfect life" for my family. However, I had no idea what kind of toll operating in this state eventually takes on the human body.

About two months after my son, Charlie, was born, I began to realize that something was wrong. Even though I'd completed my degree and was on maternity leave, I just didn't feel right. I attributed my intense feeling of fatigue to managing a newborn and a toddler—cause enough!—but when I woke up one morning covered in hives, I realized I had more than new-mom fatigue. Then I developed joint inflammation. It started in my neck and spread to my hips, knees, and wrists. I could barely make it through the day with my kids, and when my husband walked in the door each evening, I would retreat to our bedroom for the rest of the night.

After months of tests, tinkering with medication, and misdiagnosis, I found the answer: A careful doctor finally figured out that I had microscopic colitis, an autoimmune disease that affects the way the body absorbs nutrients. The stress I was experiencing had completely depleted my immune system, causing severe inflammation to my digestive system and throughout my body.

We live in a world where we expect perfection, especially from ourselves. I was determined to be the perfect mom, the perfect wife; to have the perfect house and the perfect job. And my desire to be perfect came with serious consequences. I had pushed myself to the breaking point, and it seriously affected my health and my emotional well being. This was a huge reality check for me. I knew how I wanted to feel, but in order to get there, I would need an overhaul of my lifestyle and my mentality. Something had to change.

The Price of Perfection

In my career I have worked at two schools at opposite ends of the socioeconomic spectrum: the well-off independent school just mentioned and an elementary school in a high-needs area of northwest Denver, where 95 percent of the population received a free or reduced-price lunch. At the school in northwest Denver, I vividly recall watching a young boy, José, smuggle pieces of fruit from the cafeteria into his pocket to bring home to his hungry three-year-old brother. At the well-off school, I recall a father walking into my office with his kindergartner and declaring that she *would be attending Harvard*!

When I first began my career, I believed that educating kids like José was the kind of work I wanted to do: helping those who needed it most. At the time, I equated socioeconomic status with need—that is, poorer kids needed more support. Yet at the independent school, it didn't take long for me to recognize the mental and emotional struggles the students there were facing. Just as kids in the high-need school had their own pressures and issues, the students at the independent school were some of the most anxious, stressed, depressed, and inattentive kids with whom I had ever worked. While academically they might have been achieving at a higher level, from an emotional standpoint they were no better off than José, who was uncertain where his next meal was coming from. How could this be?

Simply put, the well-off school was a pressure cooker. My husband was a teacher at the same school, and while we both thought it one of the best educational institutions in the state, we wondered, would it be the right place for our own kids? Could they handle the academic rigor? The social demands? Did we want them to struggle each evening with the hours of homework? Would they be happy there?

From that point on, we began to question whether Denver was the right place for us to raise a family. Like many families in big urban environments, we felt that we were in a rat race. My health issues were having a significant impact on our day-to-day life, but we also spent hours fighting traffic, racing from one activity to the next, caught in constant conversations about making sure our kids were in all the *right* activities—and they weren't even in kindergarten yet!

On most weekends, we would escape to our mountain getaway in search of a simpler life totally off the grid. But the weekends went by too quickly, and it wasn't much fun spending all our free time packing and unpacking for the trip with two kids under age three. So we decided to take the plunge and move back to Steamboat Springs, Colorado, the perfect small town in which to raise our family.

Changing Zip Codes Doesn't Change Everything

Before we moved, we pictured evenings spent watching sunsets, weekends camping, and our kids riding their bikes to school every day. A simpler life. Guess what? Even in small towns life gets crazy. Even in small towns you have a million activities to choose from. Even in small towns you overschedule, and you're expected to be readily accessible by phone, text, and e-mail. You still struggle to find balance, and you still have to make money. Even in small towns people get stressed out.

A few months after our move I realized that I had been trying to set up the perfect stress-free life for myself and my family *from the outside.* I had thought if I set up the perfect *external* environment—the right marriage, the right house, the right school, in the right town—we would be able to live the happy, stress-free life we were seeking.

But there is only so much you can control from the outside. No matter where you are, there will always be stressors, and if you don't have the tools *on the inside* to manage the stressors in your life, your external environment becomes irrelevant. At the high-needs public school where I worked, those kids who possessed internalized tools to handle stress and adversity did well, despite living in a tough neighborhood. At the well-off independent school, it didn't matter how swank their houses or impressive their parents' jobs; kids who didn't have the internal tools to manage stress suffered, sometimes a great deal.

Learning How to Surf: Tools of Resiliency

I find that it's a huge relief if we acknowledge—despite our different jobs, parenting styles, socioeconomic levels, or geographic locations—that we're all in this together, that we all have stress, now more than ever. As a country, we face great financial hardship. As parents, we live in a 24/7, overscheduled, overstimulated, attention-fragmented world. And our kids are not immune. They are the victims of the stress around them. Whether they are six months or sixteen, they absorb the stress of our society. What some call "acting out" may in fact be a perfectly sane reaction to an insane environment, one in which downtime has been eradicated by eternal texting and Facebook use, where the most exclusive resorts now offer technological *inaccessibility* as a high-end perk, and where a child's college future is determined (or ruined) by age eight. The good news is that the solutions for less stressed, more mindful families don't depend on creating the perfect environment for our children. We really can't control the world they grow up in to any large extent. What we *can* do is make changes to simplify their (and our) lives and help them develop tools *from the inside* to become resilient to the stress that life presents.

This book is about developing tools of resiliency. While I do address eliminating what I call "hidden stressors"—we must also acquire, and help our kids acquire, the internal mindfulness tools necessary to manage life's curveballs. I hope this book is useful for parents, grandparents, educators, and therapists. It is designed for anyone interested in helping themselves, and the children with whom they engage, to lead less stressed and more mindful lives. All the solutions are rooted in my belief that small changes can make a big difference. As mindfulness guru Jon Kabat-Zinn so artfully puts it, "You can't stop the waves, but you can learn to surf."

ONE

Generation Stress

Last summer I was preparing to make the three-hour drive back to our home in Steamboat Springs after taking the kids camping for four days with several other families. As I was packing up the car, I realized how relaxing our time in the Flat Tops Wilderness Area had been. The kids had played for hours on end in the outdoors, building forts, catching snakes and frogs, fishing, playing freeze tag, and making s'mores by the fire. There were plenty of adults around to watch the kids, so the parents were able to take turns slipping away for a hike or mountain bike ride. There'd been no fights over whose turn it was to pick the TV show, and with no cell phone service, I'd been able to disengage completely from work and other distractions. It had been easy just to be present with my family and friends.

My mood changed nearly immediately on the drive home: A small worry began to form in the pit of my stomach. First, I remembered some house repairs that had to get done; then my thoughts shifted to worrying about how we were going to juggle child care during the upcoming work week, which led to what activities I needed to sign the kids up for in the fall and how we were going to be able to afford them. In the background were the bigger stressors, such as would we ever be able to refinance our home, would our business make enough money to support us, and was my commitment to work making me a lousy mom?

As the feeling in the pit of my stomach grew, so did my level of impatience with the kids. "Stop talking to each other!" I remember screaming from the driver's seat after my previous attempts to quell their bickering had failed. "I mean it! Silence for the rest of the ride!" What had happened to the super-chill mom they had just spent four days with?

Our modern lives are drastically different from how they were a generation ago. And as our attention becomes more and more fragmented as we juggle all the roles we are cast in, and play with all the modern devices that distract us, our brains are placed in a near-constant state of stress. From an evolutionary perspective, the human brain was not designed to negotiate the stresses of today's world. It is much more at ease on a four-day camping trip with no cell phone service.

Life Is Different

It's not that adults didn't work a lot when I was growing up. They did. My dad worked hard every weekday at his job as an attorney. He'd leave the house at 7:00 A.M. sharp and return around 6:00 in the evening. When he got home, my mom would have dinner ready for us, even though she had coached my soccer practice and driven my sisters and me all over town that day. But for my dad, that was it. He'd pour a cocktail, listen to us talk about our day, and eventually make his way to the TV, where he hoped to catch a rerun of a John Wayne movie. Or he'd pick up a book and sit and read. The next day, he'd get up, retrieve the morning newspaper from the front stoop, read it (crazy, right?), then drive in to work while listening to the radio. When he walked past the receptionist, she'd hand him a slip of paper with a few messages on it, and he'd start his workday.

Today, that same attorney drives to and from work talking to clients on the phone, wakes up and reads the news on his tablet while hearing the ping of the e-mails that came in overnight, and by the time he gets to his office, is inundated with the e-mails that came in while he was in transit, from clients wondering why they have not gotten a response yet.

My mom's world would have been dramatically different today. The Saturday soccer game and one midweek practice have been replaced with a soccer club that is now a soccer business. This means she would have driven me to three practices during the week, a game an hour away on Saturday, and a tournament every other weekend. She would be inundated with e-mail reminders from teachers and school administrators, and on the way to school pickup, she would have five calls from me wondering why she was two minutes late.

The demands, the stimulation, the constant buzz—all have created, quite sadly, Generation Stress.

The reality is, I am Generation Stress. (If you read the introduction, you've probably gathered this already.) The irony is that I spend my working life researching stress and the brain, and creating solutions to help families become more resilient to the stressors in their lives. I have personally struggled with every topic presented in the pages that follow, which may have you thinking, *why would I want to take advice from* her? Certainly experience with my own stress has influenced my work, but my solutions are derived from brain science and grounded in my belief that small changes can make a big difference. I try to be intentional about practicing what I preach, and many of the solutions outlined in the chapters that follow come from trial and error in my search for ways to reduce stress and alleviate bad behaviors in my own family and in the lives of the many families I have worked with over the years.

IS IT THE KIDS OR THE PARENTS?

According to the 2010 American Psychological Association's "Stress in America Findings" report, Generation X (those of us born between 1966 and 1979) is the most stressed-out generation yet, with the effects of prolonged recession-related difficulties topping the list of things stressing us out. Add to this the modern influences of being plugged in to some device 24/7; our ridiculously demanding schedules; an ever-increasing pressure to perform, look perfect, and be perfect; and you basically have a recipe for anxiety, depression, or a total emotional breakdown.

These stressors are not impacting only us, however, and that's where our kids come in. Stress is highly contagious, so it makes sense that a generation of stressed-out parents is raising a generation of stressed-out kids. Human brains are equipped with special hardware that allows us to tap into the emotions we witness around us. This hardware comes in the form of so-called mirror neurons, which reflect the emotions we see expressed around us. Mirror neurons are the reason infants smile in response to our smiling at them. That's a lovely example, but these neurons also light up in response to other kinds of expressed emotion, not just glee.

When we see an expression on someone's face, not only do we recognize what that person is feeling, but also the area inside our brain responsible for that same emotion lights up. So if Mom is worried about something, even if she doesn't talk about it, the worry neurons inside her toddler's brain are firing as well. And if Mom is stressed, baby feels stressed, too. The good news is that positive as well as negative emotions are "catching" in this manner. So when we cultivate positive thinking and emotions in ourselves, everyone around us benefits, including our children. As more and more of us experience unprecedented levels of stress, and when the stress-associated emotions are the ones that catch and reflect back most frequently, stress makes an unprecedented impact on our mental, emotional, and physical health, and takes a significant toll on our kids.

The Down and Dirty (AKA the research)

According to research, Americans today live with moderate to high levels of stress, and struggle in their efforts to manage that stress. One in five American adults believes himself to be in poor health, and those adults who rate their health as poor report higher levels of stress. In addition to the negative affects on *their* physical health, stress affects the emotional and physical well-being of their families: "While the majority of parents don't think their children are strongly affected by stress, children report otherwise. Nearly three-quarters of parents say their stress has only a slight or no impact on their children, yet 91 percent of children report they know their parent is stressed because they observe a multitude of behaviors, such as yelling, arguing, and complaining." It should come as no surprise that children are more likely to report having a great deal of stress themselves when they have parents who live in a constant state of stress.

While so many Americans report being stressed, Generation

Xers are not only the most stressed but also the most likely to report physical symptoms of stress and to rely on unhealthy behaviors to manage their stress. More than half of Gen Xers (56 percent) report feeling irritable and angry as a result of stress, and nearly half report having headaches and feeling fatigued as a result of stress. We are also the most likely to report unhealthy behaviors—such as lying awake at night, overeating, eating unhealthy foods, skipping meals, and drinking alcohol—because of stress. While six out of ten Gen Xers report that getting enough sleep is extremely important, fewer than one in five reports doing a very good job getting enough sleep.

If you are a Gen Xer and a married woman, the news is even worse for you. Women report higher levels of stress than men, and married women report higher levels of stress than single women. In 2005 the Lucille Packard Foundation for Children's Health commissioned a series of studies that found that only 50 percent of parents rate their children's overall emotional health as excellent. Two-thirds report being extremely concerned about the well-being of their children, and 67 percent worry that their teens are too stressed. Parents have reason to be concerned. Moms are intuitive, after all. Studies show we're not worried for nothing.

Our Kids Are Paying the Price

In the course of my work, I encounter lots of kids on the edge. It didn't surprise me when I read that California college counselors have started referring to some incoming freshman as either "crispies" (kids pushed so hard they're already burned out at eighteen) or "teacups" (too fragile to exist in the world on their own). The signs show up early: levels of depression and anxiety among elementary school students are at an all-time high and continuing to rise. Nearly a third of high school students report feeling sad or hopeless. One in five school-age kids (ages eight through eighteen) has a diagnosable mental disorder—20 percent of our children! This kind of stress is incredibly dangerous, to the point where our kids' very lives are being threatened. Each year, one in five teens thinks about suicide, one in six teens makes plans for suicide, and more than one in twelve teens attempt suicide. According to one high school resource officer, the new street drug of choice among adolescents is Xanax, an antianxiety medication. This is a huge indication of how these kids are feeling. Where kids used to look for drugs to pump them up—things like speed and Ritalin—they are now looking for drugs to calm them down.

When it comes to managing stress, the APA poll indicates that children turn to sedentary behaviors when they are stressed or worried. They increasingly turn to playing video games or watching TV to relax. Unfortunately, not only do these activities actually increase stress in the brain (more on this in chapter 3), but kids who learn early in life to rely on sedentary behaviors to manage stress face serious health implications. All this for a generation of kids already experiencing rampant levels of obesity.

The Helicopter Parent Has Landed

Not only do we have a generation of stressed-out parents trying to raise kids, but how we parent our children has changed dramatically over the last generation. I used to work as an educational consultant for the Early Childhood Council in my town. One of my responsibilities was to teach social and emotional learning skills in each of the early childhood education centers. Through this work I learned a lot about each center, and I am now often called upon when parents are trying to decide where to send their child to preschool. Over and over again I hear the same thing: "I just want to make sure she is challenged," or "He already knows all his letters, so I need a place that is more academic." Since when did preschools become college-prep programs?

There was a time when the purpose of preschool was to prepare kids for kindergarten, not to allow them to skip kindergarten altogether. We want kids to enter kindergarten ready to learn. This means having strategies for getting along with others, knowing how to share and take turns, having the foundation for problem-solving skills, and being able to recognize when people feel happy or sad. Entering kindergarten ready to learn does not mean being able to read and write. In fact, for most kids, reading *is completely developmentally inappropriate* before the age of five or six. Even though we want the best for them, this early push toward academic greatness causes a great deal of stress for kids who still just want to build block towers or put on a cape.

To complicate things, we push our children to grow up more quickly in many areas while protecting them from making developmentally appropriate mistakes in others. We've gone baby-proofing crazy, making it impossible to lift a toilet seat cover without a special code and buying fifteen-foot padded fences to enclose our living rooms. We don't let our kids play with sticks or climb trees. We even put them on leashes called Kinderkords, which boast "three full feet of freedom for both you and your child." Yet it doesn't stop there. We hover over teachers, and even text them (or, worse, our kids' college professors) to let them know that Johnny forgot his homework but that we'll be running it by later. We want the best for our kids, and we want to protect them at every turn, but all this hovering and rescuing—known as helicopter parenting—has our kids thinking that making a mistake is to be avoided at all costs. We are raising perfectionists—and, by the way, that is *not* a compliment. These are kids who, at the first sign of difficulty, give up rather than try harder, for fear things won't turn out just right. Our little perfectionists are developing eating disorders, turning to drugs and alcohol to self-medicate, and are more likely than any generation before them to attempt or commit suicide. In our eagerness to keep them safe, we may actually be doing them harm.

On the one hand we are pushing our kids to excel, to learn earlier and faster than the rest, eager to carve out a place for them in this frenzied world. Yet on the other hand, we aren't allowing them to develop the skills most correlated with success: intellectual curiosity (not rote learning), creative problem-solving (which requires problems to solve), and a belief that if they keep working at something, eventually they will succeed, or at least improve. Cognitively and emotionally our children face more adversity than ever—in the form of constant stress, overscheduling, pressure to succeed, and too much screen time. All these wreak havoc on a growing brain, while denying kids the ability to form the natural cognitive defenses to buoy them in stressful times.

The Myth of "But I Turned out Okay"

We have all heard it before: "Well, when I was young I did such-and-such, and I turned out okay." At times this statement is perfectly appropriate (and comforting), but often parents do not realize the extent to which life is inherently different for kids growing up today. Life is simply not the same now as it was thirty years ago.

HOW DRASTICALLY TIMES HAVE CHANGED

It's not like we didn't watch television when we were kids.

Sure, maybe you watched *The Love Boat* on Friday nights or cartoons on Saturday. And if you missed the show, you missed it. There was no on-demand or TiVo. In 2010, the Kaiser Family Foundation, a nonprofit organization that analyzes health issues, determined that kids ages eight to eighteen spend seven hours and thirty-eight minutes per day using entertainment media—more hours per week than if it were a full-time job. And because they do so much multitasking in the form of watching television, texting, and doing homework, all at the same time, they actually manage to pack a total of *ten hours and forty-five minutes worth of media* content into those seven hours and thirty-eight minutes *per day.*

Our kids are spending *between fifty-three and seventy-five hours a week* using entertainment media alone. This is not your old TV schedule.

When I was a kid we didn't even use seat belts, and we ran wild in the neighborhood!

Parents these days don't let their tweens cross the street alone. Though studies show our kids are actually safer than ever before, we keep them on leashes, barricade them inside, and forbid their playing with anything that has a pointed end. The University of Michigan Institute for Social Research conducted a national study of 3,500 children, ages twelve and under, and found that **kids today have half as much free time as they did thirty years ago.** They don't even get playtime in school. A 2009 study conducted by researchers from the Albert Einstein College of Medicine's

Department of Pediatrics found that **only 30 percent of American students are granted adequate daily recess time.**

But across the nation kids are failing in school. They need more homework!

Every study done shows that they actually need *less*. Not only are their creative brains completely undeveloped, but they are buried under useless rote homework. In a 2005 study, 70 percent of Bay Area parents reported that their nine- to thirteen-year-olds were suffering moderate to high stress levels, with homework topping the list of stressors. Homework is consuming all their time, it's killing their love of learning, and it's taking away their childhoods. **The number one reason children over the age of eight stop reading for pleasure? Too much homework.**

I stayed up late when I was a kid. What's the big deal?

Kids who don't get enough sleep are more likely to be obese, have trouble paying attention, underperform in school, and suffer from anxiety and depression. A difference of fifteen minutes of daily sleep separates A students from B students, and Bs from Cs. **Kids sleep an average of an hour less a night than they did thirty years ago.**

There is hope. While we can't eliminate all stress, there are a lot of things we *can* do to become more resilient to the stressors in our lives. These changes don't require money, moving to the country, or quitting a job. In fact, most of my parenting lectures are more about simplifying your life rather than employing a slew of new parenting strategies. There are many simple changes we can make to help the whole family become more resilient to the stress that life presents.

Mindfulness

At the core of the solutions throughout this book are both formal and informal practices of mindfulness. Many people to whom I mention the term *mindfulness* give me a blank stare in response, as if I've just pulled out a voodoo doll.

While there are many meanings of mindfulness out there, I define it as paying attention to the present moment with kindness. Mindfulness gives us the tools not only to manage the stress that life presents but also to experience more positive emotions. Neuroscientists are finding that mindfulness changes how our brain works. In the same way we practice physical exercise to strengthen our muscles, mindfulness practice can be used to strengthen our brains! It can be performed by adults, kids, and whole families—and as we will learn in chapter 8, the results are truly profound. The practice of mindfulness could be the single most effective way to improve your parenting, your relationships, your health, and to increase your happiness in general.

The formal practice of mindfulness in the United States was translated from Buddhist teachings by Jon Kabat-Zinn, who created a secular program for people with chronic pain and stress in the 1970s. Since its inception, mindfulness has helped the people who practice it exhibit greater self-confidence, be more outgoing, and feel more grateful for their lives. They are healthier, have stronger immune systems, and exhibit less stress, aggression, anxiety, and depression. In fact they experience fewer negative emotions in general. They are simply happier.

While mindfulness is most commonly practiced by adults, I have found it to be a particularly effective technique for children. In fact, when I started teaching mindfulness skills to the students in preschools, I found the effects so powerful that I gave up my private psychology practice to create my own unique method for teaching mindfulness to children.

One of the beauties of using mindfulness in a classroom setting is that it positively impacts *all* kids. It helps kids who struggle with behavior and attention deficits, and it helps kids who may be at the high end academically but who struggle with perfectionism, anxiety, or obstacles to reaching their potential. I now spend a great deal of my time traveling around the country showing parents and teachers how to integrate mindfulness into their homes and classrooms. I'm finding that when kids learn these skills, they demonstrate significant improvement in attention, impulse control, ability to regulate emotions, and development of empathy. The benefits to this practice are extensive and very real.

If the term *mindfulness* sounds too esoteric to you, let me say that regardless of whether you've ever set foot in a yoga studio or sat on a meditation cushion, you likely engage in informal mindfulness practices without even realizing it. Informal mindfulness happens when you feel completely engaged in present moment-to-moment awareness, when you completely lose track of time because you're so involved with what you're doing. I'll give you an example. At eleven o'clock on a typical Sunday evening in our town, dozens of middle-aged men and women descend upon the ice rink to play in the coed recreational hockey league. They play for a couple of hours and then return home at one o'clock in the morning, are lucky to be asleep by two, and have to wake up in time to get to work the next morning. It seems crazy to most people that anyone would want to start off their work week in this way, but if you ask any of them why they do it, they will say that when they play, they feel completely present and engaged in the game. They aren't rehashing all the tasks they forgot to do that day or what they need to do tomorrow. They are 100 percent present in skating and following that puck, and that feels great!

You likely already engage in an activity that makes you feel this way. For me, it's playing soccer. For my husband, it's fishing and skiing. For others, it might be gardening, cooking, or praying.

We spend too much time in our minds revisiting the past or rehearsing for the future. Mindfulness is an exercise in paying attention to the here and now, something that in modern times is incredibly hard to do. While informal mindfulness activities make you feel good in the moment, when you practice mindfulness *formally*—this might include performing a sitting meditation or engaging in mindful breathing, mindful listening, or mindful eating—it brings that moment-to-moment awareness into your daily life. There is no one right way to do it, and mindfulness practice can be tailored to fit different lives. The importance lies in actually making the practice a regular part of your life.

For parents, practicing mindfulness doesn't just lead to decreased stress and increased pleasure in parenting, but also brings profound benefits to kids. A University of California–Los Angeles study showed that parents who practiced mindfulness for one year were dramatically more satisfied and felt more successful as parents, even though they learned no new parenting-specific skills. Over the course of the year-long study, participants' kids showed the effects of having more mindful parents. They didn't fight as much with their siblings, and they were less aggressive and more sociable.

Here is an example of how mindfulness has worked for my family. It was the glorious start to summer, and I was on a hike with my six-year-old daughter, Macy. Ours was a perfect setting in the mountains of Steamboat Springs, Colorado, yet my daughter could not stop complaining that she was too tired to walk "all the way to the pond" and that she might get stung by a bee and that she had pebbles in her shoe, as well as every other grievance she could claim. It took every ounce of effort on my part not to say "screw it!" and return to the car, never to take her on a hike again. Somehow—and this didn't come easily—I decided to try to take a more mindful approach. I told her that I needed her to help me with some of my work. This piqued her interest. What ensued amazed and inspired me.

When I talk to young kids about mindfulness I often talk about how we have all kinds of seeds in our brains: seeds of anger, sadness, jealousy, and disappointment. We also have seeds of peace and happiness. Just as in a real garden, the seeds that grow and flourish are the ones to which we pay attention. So, which seeds do you want to grow: seeds of peace and happiness or seeds of discontent? Like me, my daughter's natural tendency is to pay attention to those seeds of discontent, so changing that took some effort.

I asked my daughter how we might be able to practice mindfulness (a concept with which she is familiar) on our hike. She answered, "We can practice it by paying attention to all the things around us right now." We then took a seat on a rock and just listened to the sounds around us. We heard the river flowing, birds chirping, dogs running along the trail. Macy was certain she could even hear the sounds of butterfly wings!

We then decided to pay attention to all the things we could see. We noticed the details in the wildflowers that were blooming. We looked at the patterns of the veins in the petals, and we noticed that some flowers hung upside down and some opened to the sky to soak in the sun. We smelled the flowers. We noticed the aroma of the pine trees and the odor of wet dogs. We then started to search for rocks we could skip across the pond. We scoured every inch of the trail trying to find the perfect skipping stones.

By the end of our hike, not only had we walked twice as far as we originally intended, but a major shift had occurred in both our moods. Macy mentioned that she thought she had taken good care of her seeds of peace and happiness and that she could feel them growing inside her mind. While my intention had been to change her behavior and not to change my mood, I noticed how much more relaxed and peaceful I felt.

We're lucky to have the wilderness at our doorstep, but mindfulness doesn't have to come courtesy of a hike in the woods. Take a moment to appreciate the pattern of falling raindrops against the car window, pay attention to the slow rise and fall of your breath, or point out the rising or setting sun to your child and watch its brilliant ascent or descent together. Just as it did for Macy and me, the act of noticing will itself bring powerful and positive changes.

How to Use This Book

My hope in writing this book is to illuminate the myriad ways we live stressed lives, and pass those lives on to our children, and then **tell you what you can do about it.** The take-away is this: You have the power to make changes that will drastically affect your family's stress level and overall happiness and literally set your child's brain on a new course! With that in mind, there are several ways you can use this book.

I chose some of the most common and troublesome areas that affect our stress levels in modern times, from lack of sleep to too much screen time. While reading the book from cover to cover will give you the most complete picture and the widest variety of solutions, each subject has its own chapter, in case you need help in one area *right now*. I still recommend you read part 1 for a thorough grounding in the issue at hand and to get a primer on cognitive function before skipping to any of the later chapters. When we understand the brain, it empowers us and our children to recognize stress, how it impacts our minds and bodies, and to better recognize what we can do to minimize its effects.

After part 1, the book is organized into two sections. Part 2 focuses on external stressors, the things we can adjust and that are, to a greater extent, within our control. While this section does not provide instruction for a formal mindfulness practice, it is intended to help us eliminate common obstacles that prevent us from living mindful lives.

Part 3 gives a detailed introduction to the concept of mindfulness, dives deeper into the formal practice of mindfulness, and provides a guide to help you create a mindful family. It contains strategies for increasing yours and your kids' resiliency to the stress that life inevitably presents. I've arranged the book so that adults seeking guidance with a certain issue—such as their kids' getting too little sleep or too much screen time—can read through the first two chapters for an introduction to brain chemistry and then go straight to the chapter of interest. There you'll find a clear description of what is happening in a child's brain when she's, say, chronically sleep deprived or in front of a computer four hours a day.

At the conclusion of every chapter (beginning with chapter 3), you will find dozens of solutions for you and your family. Where appropriate, I break the solutions down by age group. For pre-kindergartners (referred to as "young children"), for example, a better sleep routine might counterintuitively include inserting a little more creative playtime in their day. For teens, rechanneling their technology bug might take the form of having them put together playlists for the dinner hour or your commute. You may then revisit different sections as your children grow and their needs and issues shift and change. You may also want to visit the step-by-step guide to creating a mindful family, chapter 9, for solutions and mindfulness techniques that will work for all ages.

One final note: While I provide dozens of solutions in each chapter, my intention is not for you to try all of them. (That would be stressful!) Choose one or two that resonate with you and try those. When they become routine, add some more. All families are different, and the breadth of solutions is meant to accommodate a variety of needs. The idea is to find the solutions that can make a difference for *your* family.

TWO

The Stress Response in the Brain

magine this all-too-familiar scenario. You are at your desk, entering the last few numbers into a spreadsheet. Glancing at the time on your monitor, you start typing faster; you're already running late to meet with an important client. You finish! Now you need only print out two copies of the spreadsheet and you'll be on your way. Keys in hand, you click Print and . . . your computer freezes. You move the mouse frantically, click again and again. Nothing moves. You didn't save your changes, you don't have time to reboot the computer and start all over again, and no matter how many times you desperately click that mouse, the cursor doesn't budge. You can imagine the words that might come out of your mouth in such a scenario, but it's more important, and more revealing, to take a peek behind the scenes and look at what would be happening in your brain.

Our modern lives have evolved rapidly to a place and pace that feel wildly different from those of families living even just a generation ago. In the last chapter, we talked about how our 24/7 existence affects our social structures, our stress levels, and our physical and emotional health. In my work researching how the

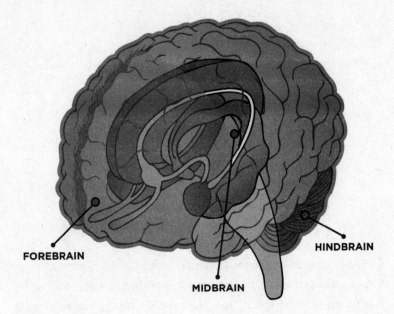

FOREBRAIN

HINDBRAIN

MIDBRAIN

brain functions and responds to stress, I deal with the physiological absolutes of our brain chemistry, investigating the structures in our brains that have not yet evolved to match our modern world. Having that information helps us understand our reactions to external stress, and helps us work to reduce the number of false alarms that keep our bodies in a near-constant state of stress.

In the simplest of terms, your brain has three sections: the hindbrain, the midbrain, and the forebrain. Within each of those sections are several structures with specific functions.

The **hindbrain** contains the cerebellum, medulla, and pons, and is fairly primitive, by which I mean it covers basic functions such as breathing, balance, heart rate, digestion, and movement (even sneezing). You don't consciously will your heart to beat, nor your lungs to breathe—it just happens. Your body is governed effectively by your hindbrain to operate on a basic level.

The **midbrain** is a small section of the brain primarily in charge of processing auditory and visual information.

The primary focus of this book, however, is the **forebrain,** which is the biggest part of our brain and the most advanced. It's where we develop language and where higher thought and reasoning occur. It's the part of the brain that makes us human—and as such, the reason we evolved to be the leaders of the animal kingdom. If you can't be the biggest or the strongest, you'd better be the smartest, and we have our forebrains to thank for our continued survival on this planet. Yet our forebrains are also responsible for complex physiological reactions that in modern times can result in chronic anxiety, worry, stress, and depression in adults and their kids.

Within the forebrain is the limbic system, comprised of the thalamus, hypothalamus, hippocampus, and amygdala. The limbic system is the part of our brain that deals with emotions and memories through a series of complex and, frankly, amazing processes.

What's Happening in the Brain

Messages travel through our brain by first passing through the thalamus, a sort of triage station. The thalamus figures out where to route the sensory information as it receives it. If the information is perceived as unfamiliar or threatening, the brain signals the amygdala (pronounced *a-MIG-dah-lah*) to act.

The amygdala is a little "fire alarm" in the limbic system, located toward the middle of the brain. It's just one inch long, but it packs a powerful wallop. Its job is to respond to situations that are unfamiliar, emotionally charged, dangerous, exciting, or painful.

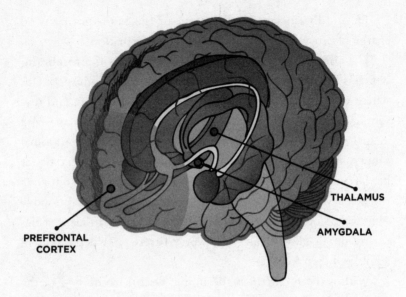

PREFRONTAL
CORTEX

THALAMUS

AMYGDALA

That's an important function: It activates a set of responses meant to promote survival.

If you're crossing a busy intersection and you notice a speeding car hurtling toward you, your amygdala kicks off a set of responses designed to save your life. The first response is to block your parasympathetic nervous system (PNS) and activate your sympathetic nervous system (SNS). Your PNS is the one in charge when you're not in danger or, in modern times, when you're not under stress. (Think of lying on the beach with a good book.) Because of its main functions, the PNS is sometimes called the "rest-and-digest" system. When your parasympathetic nervous system is operating, your heart rate slows and your blood pressures decreases. Your body is able to tend to basic "chores" such as digesting food, eliminating waste, and even engaging in acts of reproduction.

I don't need to tell you that when stress kicks in, sex is one of the first things to go straight out the window. Now your SNS is in

A host of chemicals, hormones, and peptides affect the brain in different ways. What follows are those I refer to in this book and the general effects they produce in our bodies.

NEUROTRANSMITTERS AND HORMONES

* **Serotonin** is a natural antidepressant that works to regulate and affect our moods, sleep, digestion, aggression, and pain.
* **Dopamine** is released as part of the reward system of the brain, giving people a natural incentive to do things such as have sex or eat chocolate. It is a key player in motivation, addiction, and pleasure as well as influencing our ability to pay attention.
* **Norepinephrine** arouses and alerts us and is important for sleeping, dreaming, and learning.
* **Acetylcholine** promotes active learning and wakefulness.
* **Opioids** occur naturally to soothe and reduce pain and to provide a stress buffer in the brain.
* **Oxytocin** is most well known for promoting in us a "mothering," or nurturing, instinct toward children and our partners; women have higher levels than do men.
* **Vasopressin** helps support intimacy between couples (known in clinical terms as pair bonding) and, in men, may promote aggression toward sexual rivals.

NEUROCHEMICALS

* **Cortisol** can be both "good" and "bad," depending on its concentration. It is released by the adrenal glands during the stress response, and may either inhibit or excite the hippocampus. It is also associated with weight gain and other health problems.
* **Estrogen** is present in both men's and women's brains in different amounts and affects libido, mood, and memory.

control, and in charge of keeping you alive. Your body goes on emergency alert. Digestion halts. The stomach and intestines stop absorbing nutrients. Your body doesn't even waste energy salivating, creating that dry mouth you feel when you're nervous. Your body is bathed in stress hormones, including adrenaline and cortisol. Your nervous system releases epinephrine (adrenaline) and norepinephrine (noradrenaline), along with more than thirty other hormones meant to get you focused and alert and in survival mode. This is the classic "fight, flight, or freeze" response. The effects within your body are instantaneous and profound, and they work. You sprint toward the curb and avoid getting hit by that inattentive driver's car.

FIGHT, FLIGHT, OR FREEZE

As soon as you saw that car, a flood of stress hormones enacted changes in your body. What follows are the common sensations we recognize as being associated with fear, danger, and stress:

+ You may feel cold because the blood vessels in your skin have constricted, routing the blood toward your major organs, to keep them functioning, and to your muscles, so you'll be able to escape more quickly.
+ Your blood pressure increases and your heart rate speeds up, likely causing a "pounding" feeling in your chest.
+ Your muscles tense up, readying you for a fight or preparing you to run.
+ Your breathing rate increases and your breath deepens, to provide your tissues with more oxygen.
+ Your pupils dilate, to focus and improve your vision.
+ You begin to sweat, ensuring your body doesn't overheat with the exertion of battle or flight.

✦ Your hands and feet may feel cold and clammy as blood is diverted away from your extremities. That way you're less likely to bleed to death if you're injured.

✦ Also, to protect you from the effects of injury, you become less sensitive to pain.

✦ You may feel a choking sensation or tightness in your chest due to the increased breathing rate.

✦ You may feel dizzy or lightheaded, or experience feelings of unreality (as if you're watching a movie instead of your life), because blood flow to your brain is inhibited.

✦ You have difficulty concentrating on other tasks that might distract you from the immediate danger at hand.

We all recognize this fight, flight, or freeze response, and it makes perfect sense when it comes to keeping us alive. But what about the rest of the time?

Our Life-or-Death Lives

Fight, flight, or freeze goes back to our caveman days, and made a lot more sense then, when life was mostly about making sure animals didn't tear us and our families limb from limb while we slept. It also makes sense in modern times when there is real danger. You want your amygdala to sound that alarm and get your body ready for action if you need to jump out of the way of that car, or deal with an intruder in the middle of the night, or lift a heavy object off a loved one, or freeze when your boss scans the room for volunteers to speak at this year's annual conference.

When this stress response is working properly, it's a magnificent system. It helps you stay focused, energetic, and alert. The downside of this system is that, at times, it overrides the rational parts of your brain—specifically, the prefrontal cortex, or what I like to refer to simply as the "smart part" of your brain. The prefrontal cortex is the executive processing area of the brain. It helps you pay attention, control your impulses, solve problems, and think about the consequences of your decisions. It is also where most classroom learning occurs. The prefrontal cortex is critical for guiding our day-to-day functioning. We run into trouble when our prefrontal cortex does not function in healthy and productive ways.

THE BEAR AND ME

We now know the physiological effects of the stress response, which range from sweating to heart pounding to superhuman adrenaline surges. I'd like to share my own experience with a real-life fight, flight, or freeze situation to demonstrate what happens to our prefrontal cortex when the stress response kicks into gear. Several years ago I was riding my mountain bike through the woods on a narrow, single-track trail near my home, alone. Well, I *thought* I was alone, until I came up over a ridge and encountered a large black bear only about fifteen feet in front of me and heading my direction. I locked my brakes, and the bike came to a screeching halt. I froze. The bear reared up on its hind legs.

I've lived in the mountains on and off for more than a decade; I know *exactly* what you're supposed to do when you see a bear. You're supposed to back away slowly while speaking in a nonthreatening voice. If you're on a bike, as I was, you're supposed to dismount and hold the bike over your head, making yourself appear larger than you are, all the while speaking in a soothing tone, and backing away.

What do you suppose I did?

I stared at that bear, and it stared back at me. Then I flipped my bike around and rode it as fast as I possibly could back up the mountain. Luckily for me, the bear seemed to be suffering its own prefrontal crisis. Instead of giving chase and making a meal out of me, it turned and ran in the opposite direction.

That day I could have ridden fifty more miles thanks to the adrenaline rush my body's flight response gave me. When I finally was able to breathe and think normally again, I was disappointed with myself, for allowing my amygdala to overtake the rational part of my brain. I had *known* how to handle the situation correctly, but all those rational, forward-thinking thoughts were in my prefrontal cortex, the part of my brain that was completely overpowered by my desire to flee. In that moment, the alarm had been so strong that I couldn't use logic, because I couldn't access it. I had only instinct and a base fear response to guide me.

But normally, there's no bear . . .

The Chronic Stress Response

Even in Steamboat Springs, our bear sightings are few and far between. And that's the problem with the fight, flight, or freeze response: In modern life, more often than not, our PNS gets triggered unnecessarily by events that are hardly life-threatening. Remember how your computer was crashing at the beginning of this chapter, and you were going to be late for your meeting? For most of us, that situation would trigger nearly the same neurological and physical reaction as my encounter with the bear. Of course the response is wasted. Are you going to run away from your living room or do battle with your laptop? No, you just want the @#$%# file to print. But in a brain that is often stressed, the nuances are lost, and a full stress reaction kicks into gear. And not only is that stress response wasted—fight, flight, or freeze won't help with the modern-day problematic printer—but it may also do you harm.

The file won't print. In reaction, your heart speeds up and your blood pressure spikes; you panic and lose any ability to concentrate and figure out what to do. Your body's response makes it harder for you to use your prefrontal cortex, the smart part of your brain, to solve the problem at hand in a rational manner. The bigger problem is that our contemporary environment puts our brain in a *frequent* state of fight, flight, or freeze, often without our even realizing it. And that's the thing about today's stress: Our brains are not equipped to handle a constant influx of stress responses. They are stuck in the Paleolithic era. Mentally, we're still cavemen.

The caveman brain needed that extreme fight, flight, or freeze response to be at the ready, because his survival was much more tenuous on a day-to-day basis. We modern humans, who are not often required to spear wild boar to feed our families or traverse jungle terrain to find shelter, could do with a less trigger-happy amygdala, but our brains haven't gotten the evolutionary message.

Figure 2.1 illustrates how the stress response is supposed to work in our daily lives. At the bottom is our baseline. When we are here we feel calm and at ease. Our prefrontal cortex is working efficiently. We can pay attention to the people around us, we are focused, we make clear decisions, and we can solve problems. When we are in high alert, up at the peak of the graph, our limbic system is stimulated. We are in fight, flight, or freeze mode. We are reactive, impulsive, forgetful, and we tend to feel scattered and overwhelmed.

You'll notice that we don't stay at the top of the graph after a stress event. Imagine we are prehistoric hunters and gatherers and are out on a walk looking for food. We see a snake—*spike!*—and

Figure 2.1 The Normal Stress Response

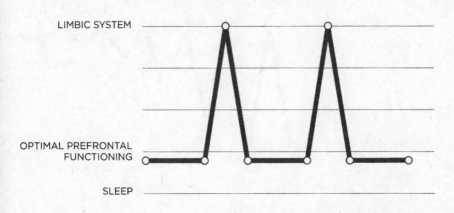

the stress response is triggered. Then we realize it is only a stick, not a snake. With no danger, things go back to a balanced state. A few days later a pack of wolves surrounds the tribe. *Spike!* We scare them away, and our system goes back to a balanced state.

Now look at Figure 2.2, which represents a chronic stress response; this is why we are "Generation Stress." Remember at the beginning of the chapter when your computer froze? *Spike!* Things have just begun to calm down when you receive a call from the school. Your child has a suspected case of strep throat and needs to be picked up immediately. *Spike!* You arrive home after a visit to the doctor—where you spent a full hour in the waiting room, before standing in line at the pharmacy for *another* twenty minutes for antibiotics—when your spouse calls to say an out-of-town client is coming over for dinner. *Spike!* You have nothing in the fridge, and your house is a disaster. While cleaning the house and trying to soothe your sick kid, you see a disturbing story on the news—*spike!*—and you're so overwhelmed

Figure 2.2 Chronic Stress Response

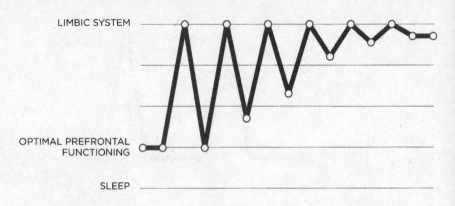

you leave the house late and are the last one to pick up your youngest kid from child care. *Spike!*

When our life is like this more frequently than not, our baseline shifts, hovering much closer to a near-constant state of fight, flight, or freeze. You may refer to what you feel as " too busy" or just "stressed," but there is a physiological reason behind feeling reactive, impulsive, overwhelmed, and scattered. When you lose the ability to easily access your prefrontal cortex, you have difficulty thinking clearly and being attentive to the people around you. You are unable to be thoughtful in your responses, and have trouble staying focused. Your ability to solve problems is diminished.

Stressors both large and small stimulate the stress response in children as well as in adults. For example, the stress response is activated in the child who fears abuse (a potentially life-or-death situation), and also in the child worried about failing a math test (not critical for survival). The items in Table 2.1 have been shown to trigger a stress response:

ADULTS	KIDS
Receiving late-night phone calls or texts	Hearing about natural disasters—tornadoes, fires, earthquakes, etc.
Trying to interpret the tone of a text or e-mail	Trying to interpret the tone of a text or e-mail
Being late	Being late
Forgetting things	Being embarrassed in front of classmates
Losing something	Separating from a parent
Hearing creaks and "bumps in the night"	Getting bullied
Getting stuck in traffic	Breaking a toy
Watching the news	Taking a test at school
Having something in the house or car break down	Doing homework
Speaking in public	Playing video games
Thinking about your to-do list	Watching TV (of any kind)
Being spread too thin	Being overscheduled
Multitasking	Being afraid of the dark
Fighting with a partner or co-worker	Hearing parents fight
Worrying about finances	Worrying about the family's finances

Table 2.1. Fight, Flight, or Freeze Triggers

As you can see, Table 2.1 is full of . . . well, life. You know what this constant stress feels like for you, but how do you recognize it when it's happening in your kid?

The Effects of Stress on Kids

You've gone to watch your daughter's second-grade play. She's a tree, but she has a speaking part, and the two of you have been practicing her lines in the car and evenings before bed. She's been totally hamming it up; she's got her part down cold. You even created a fabulous costume, complete with moving "leaves" that shimmer as she walks. You settle into your seat, chat with nearby parents, and get your video camera ready. Her cue music starts, and she sidles her roots out onto the stage. Then, as you begin to move your lips, soundlessly reciting her lines, you are horrified to see her standing as still as the tree she is playing. Her mouth isn't moving; she's frozen in abject terror. Her lips don't move; her eyes don't blink. You notice the rush of red to her cheeks and the sweat as it pops out on her brow. In the glare of the lights, and with the rustle of the audience and the sight of the hundred parents out to watch the show, with all the pressure to shine and make you and her teacher and her classmates proud, she is . . . totally frozen.

When I give talks to parents, I usually illustrate this moment with a clip of Ralphie from *A Christmas Story,* specifically the moment when he tries to ask Santa for a Red Ryder BB Gun and freezes, but you can imagine it happening in any number of ways—when your child is taking a test, or pitching in the baseball game and just can't throw a strike, or giving a speech, or asking someone to the prom. A less obvious but more common stress response might be triggered when a child sees a violent commercial while watching his favorite sports team play. Children are as prone to the activation of the fight, flight, or freeze response as we are, and they have just as many opportunities in the day for it to interfere with their lives.

Unfortunately, some parents interpret their kids' behavior as their being bratty or defiant, or having ADHD, when in fact they're showing signs of chronic cumulative stress. The symptoms may include:

✦ Mood swings
✦ Problems with attention and concentration
✦ Anxiety
✦ Aggression
✦ Overreaction to minor problems
✦ Depression
✦ Memory problems
✦ Digestive problems
✦ Weakened immune system
✦ Sleep disruptions

The Effects of Stress on Adults

In adults, chronic stress leads to a host of problems, including a lack of interest in sex. That's right. It's not about being too busy or tired. Just as the digestive system's being halted frequently by stress can cause long-term constipation, the sex hormones' being shut off too many times while you're in "survival" mode can affect your long-term interest in sex.

When we experience a lot of stress, our brains become conditioned to interpret even minor disturbances as life threatening.

This sets off a hormonal chain reaction. An abundance of the stress hormone cortisol will be released, which can lead to obesity, high blood pressure, and a host of other health problems. In fact, studies show that 75 to 90 percent of doctor's visits are for health problems caused or exacerbated by stress. Stress harms every bodily system we have. We know what short-term stress feels like in our bodies. What you might not know is that continuous stress produces significant changes in our brains.

The Long-Term Effects of the Stress Response

To illustrate the long-term effects of habitual fight, flight, or freeze mode, I like to ask people to imagine sledding down a hill. When you first set out, it's early morning. The snow has just stopped falling, so it's fresh, and you're the first person to go down the hill. What happens? Your sled goes about two feet and then stops. Then you have to stomp back up to the top and push yourself down a little farther, and a little farther still. There's no slick pathway yet—you have to keep going over that same spot several times to pack down the snow and make it smooth so you can sled over it all the way down to the bottom.

Now take that same hill after kids have been sledding down it for hours, and you're going to have a much different experience— your sled is going to race down that hill so fast you'll get windburn. Building neural pathways in the brain operates in a similar fashion: The more often a pathway is used, the easier it is to zoom down it. With repeated use, certain neural pathways in our brain become wrapped in a layer of myelin (a kind of lubrication). This optimizes these pathways, making them more like a broadband cable Internet connection and less like dial-up.

The more frequently your brain engages in a particular way, the more likely it is to do so again. In brain terms, the more you light up the pathway from the thalamus to the amygdala, triggering that fight, flight, or freeze response, the more likely it is for the brain to use that pathway even when it's not appropriate. Your brain is more likely to choose that path, at the slightest provocation, when your computer freezes or when someone cuts you off in traffic. The physiological effects are the same. Your brain no longer is used to functioning appropriately and using the "right" pathways, so it defaults to the ones it uses most often. And without some changes, that's the way it will stay.

The Vietnam Vet and Your Kids

An MRI scan of a Vietnam veteran with post-traumatic stress disorder (PTSD) (with symptoms including difficulty concentrating, hostility, anxiety, and depression) would show that the majority of his brain activity occurs in the limbic system (the "alarm" part) instead of in the prefrontal cortex. It's likely that his brain developed this pattern in Vietnam, when he was in constant fear for his life, and these patterns continued long after he returned home safely.

This person is likely to overreact even to minor annoyances and changes—he's the guy who might try to run you off the road because you used your turn signal too late. Because he spent so much time in fight, flight, or freeze mode while at war, his brain became wired to set off the alarm much more quickly and more frequently than the brains of people who haven't had his type of experiences.

In fact, many combat veterans, police officers, and survivors of childhood abuse with PTSD show structural changes in their brains. Their brain scans likely look very similar to the scan of the Vietnam vet. Recent research has shown that someone doesn't have to experience a major trauma to show the same kind of symptoms as PTSD. Kids and adults who experience a whole lot of "little" stressors can have the same kind of brain patterns as our Vietnam vet. In short, there are several ways to arrive at the same problem: Experience one traumatic act or period of extreme stress that's so severe it hurls your sled right down that hill, or experience a slow buildup of lots of small stressors over time that carve out that slick pathway down the same route—or a combination of the two. Remember that old anti-drug ad, "This is your brain on drugs"? Well, this is your brain on constant stress.

The Isolated Brain

It so happens that there is an additional evolutionary component to our ability to manage chronic stress. Just as our stress response is exaggerated in relation to our modern-day needs, our built-in coping mechanism—in the form of empathy and the way we relate to one another as humans, groups, and families—is being challenged like never before.

In the same way that we can trace the evolution of our "caveman" brains and see why they trigger our stress response, we can also look at the natural safeguards our bodies developed to help us manage our responses to stress appropriately. You might not be surprised to learn that those natural safeguards involve interacting with other people. Humans are social creatures; we evolved living in large groups. Our earliest brain development is designed to help us cope with everyday stressors. Simply put, we need other people to help us cope with stress, both as adults and as children.

In *Born for Love: Why Empathy Is Essential—and Endangered,* child psychiatrist Bruce D. Perry and science journalist Maia Szalavitz describe how the first interactions between mother and baby shape the neural systems of the stress response happening inside our bodies, allowing mother and child to "self-regulate," or cope with stress internally. Cells inside our brain called mirror neurons respond in the same way whether our body performs an action or we watch that action being performed. Mirror neurons are responsible for newborn babies' ability to copy some facial expressions: When Mama smiles, baby smiles. Mirror neurons are also the reason babies cry when they hear other babies cry—the babies can't tell the difference between the other babies' being upset and their being so. The simple act of reflecting expressions belies what Perry and Szalavitz call "a highly sophisticated neural capability," and it's in mirroring that we first develop empathy, or our ability to feel *with* someone in difficult circumstances rather than just feeling bad *for* them in a more detached way.

Little things such as mothers talking to babies or gazing at them while they breastfeed, or seemingly meaningless acts such as a four-year-old spending twenty seconds looking into the eyes of an adult, prompt a physiological response. Our brains fire up the mirror neurons when we talk to the barista preparing our coffee, or brush up against someone on the bus, or play with another kid on the playground. These are all forms of "face time" that are important for teaching us empathy. But what happens when that face time starts to erode, when we shift, in evolutionary terms, from tribes to a state of near isolation?

From the time when we lived in hunter-gatherer clans of about forty people (clans that featured a high ratio of adults to children), humans have moved toward increased isolation. Nearly two hundred years ago in Western society we were down to living in average multigenerational groups of ten, a number that was halved by the 1960 census, which showed average households of five. Now fewer than three people live in the average American household.

Not only are we now not surrounded by different generations of humans or even groups of humans at all, but when we are in groups, we spend our time interacting with screens rather than with one another! We retire to our bedrooms, probably to type e-mails or send text messages. We rarely share family meals. Kids pass their days in groups of more than thirty with only one adult. From an evolutionary standpoint, I love how Dr. Bruce Perry, author of *Born for Love,* puts it: Our brains find this new situation "so biologically disrespectful it's incomprehensible." This transition from multigenerational, engaged homes to isolation, hiding behind computer screens, explains our spiraling inability to manage chronic stress. It's not just that we feel more isolated; our brains do not have the relational environment they need to develop appropriate responses to regulate stress.

People living in larger groups with more face-to-face interactions are constantly sorting through issues created by the group dynamic. Imagine a family of four with different dinnertime chores. Some nights, one child is not going to get the chore—say, setting the table—that he wants the most. This child, who didn't get his wish because he is living in this engaged family, has to sort through his disappointment to remain part of the conversation and the dynamic of the family dinner table. When faced with disappointment in a classroom environment, this same child will have the experience and tools to fall back on to remain connected to the teacher and the material being taught. Without these face-to-face interactions we are simply left with a stress response and all of the most primitive fight, flight, or freeze characteristics that go along with it.

Is there Such a Thing as Good Stress?

We can't eliminate stress from our lives; nor would we want to—some degree of stress is actually necessary and beneficial for us. If we never had any "practice stress," we'd be clueless about how to react in the case of a real danger. We'd also be so laid back that we probably wouldn't ever strive for greatness; we would not have people out there working to cure cancer, invent new technology systems, or solve environmental disasters.

There is some "good stress" inherent in learning new things, trying out new skills, meeting new people, pushing yourself, and so on. Physiologically, small amounts of stress can boost memory and immune function. When parents protect their children from "good stress," the kids don't get to practice reacting when something negative happens, and as a consequence, they're unable to handle difficult situations. You want your child to reach her potential, which means taking risks on expanding her boundaries by doing "stressful" things—playing her first softball game, singing in the school talent show, taking the SATs, and applying for college. For adolescents especially, this type of good stress becomes a biological imperative. We just can't let it get out of control.

Unavoidable and Avoidable Stressors

We can't prevent our kids' beloved dog from dying, we can't pull them out of school every time someone says something nasty to them, and we can't get them excused from taking tests because it's stressing them out. These (and other items in the left-hand column of Table 2.2) are unavoidable stressors. There are, however, many things that cause kids stress (such as the items in the right-hand column of Table 2.2) that we *can* control or help our kids to control as they get older.

By either eliminating these stressors or providing kids with the tools to deal with them—such as increased face time with peers or parents—we can make them much more resilient to the unavoidable stressors in their lives. In the chapters that follow, I will outline specific tools parents can use with children of different ages, from pre-K to teens, to help them become more resilient to stress.

While the next few chapters speak quite a bit about removing "hidden stressors" from our children's lives, the key to stress management is not necessarily removing stress, but rather, building tools and strategies to manage it. Children should use the same skills to handle "good stress" as they do to handle "bad stress." Kids as young as three years old can begin to acquire such tools, and what a gift we are giving them to handle all that life will throw their way!

A great way to start is by teaching kids exactly what is happening in their brains when something stressful occurs, giving them the children's version of the response I outline for you at the beginning of this chapter.

UNAVOIDABLE STRESSORS	AVOIDABLE STRESSORS
Experiencing a divorce in the family	Being late
Moving	Rushing from one activity to the next
Having problems with peers	Not getting enough sleep
Being bullied	Watching too much TV
Having a pet die	Playing too many video games
Experiencing a parent's illness	Having a routine disrupted
Losing a favorite toy	Seeing events on the news
Experiencing the death of a loved one	Doing homework
Being called on in class	Being consumed with social status
Taking tests	Feeling pressure to perform

Table 2.2. Common Unavoidable and Avoidable Stressors

Teaching Your Kids About Their Brains

I often give talks to young children about the stress response—but of course I don't describe it in exactly the same terms that I would use with adults. It empowers them to have some understanding of the mechanisms at work. As with adults, when kids start to understand that what is happening inside their brain is a physiological reaction—the same as their stomach hurting after they eat too much ice cream—they also begin to understand that they have some say over that reaction. As a consequence, their emotions don't seem so beyond their control. In fact, I find that kids' understanding of their bodies, and their connection to how their bodies feel, is very intuitive, sometimes more so than adults'.

With that in mind, here's how I teach them; you may want to explain it to your kids this way, too.

The Stress Response Explained for Older Kids

You have a smart part and an alarm part in your brain. I want you to put your hand up to your forehead. There, in the front part of your brain, is the smart part. It's called the prefrontal cortex. That's the part that helps you pay attention, solve problems, and make good choices.

Now I want you to put your hand on the back of your head. Back there is the amygdala, which is very small and very powerful. It's like an alarm that can set off a little fire inside your brain. Not a real fire, but it can feel that way, because when that alarm goes off, it is like your mind is filled with smoke and it becomes difficult to use the smart part of your brain to make a good decision.

The Stress Response Explained for Young Children

Imagine you're in your room building a tower out of blocks. You're about to set the record for the biggest tower that's ever been built at your house. You just have one more block to put on the top, and you're so excited to show your parents this amazing tower you've built. Then, just as you're about to put that last block on, your little sister or your dog comes in and, by accident, knocks down the whole thing. You might be so mad or frustrated that it sets off the alarm in your brain, and you might want to do something like hit or kick or scream or cry or run away. Because the alarm set off the fire, the smoke filling your brain doesn't let you think that your sister or your dog didn't mean to do it, or that if you built the tower once you can build it again.

For older kids, I simply change the example to something relevant for them. For early elementary, it might be that they built a fort or a LEGO ship. For tweens, it could be that they arrived in class and realized they left an important homework assignment or their lunch at home by the front door, or accidentally e-mailed the wrong person. For teens, it may be that they sat down to take a crucial final exam and went totally blank on the answers to the first three questions, or someone tagged them in a really embarrassing photo on Facebook.

Bringing in the Tools

There's a way we can put that fire out, though.

Have you ever been to a birthday party? A lot of time, at a party, there's a cake with candles. On top of the candle is a little fire. How do you put that fire out? By blowing on it. We can put the fire in our brain out in the same way, by using our breath.

Close your eyes and think about how frustrated and angry you might feel after someone knocked down your tower. Now I want you to take three deep breaths. Put your hand in front of your nose and feel the air as you take a deep breath in through your mouth and then slowly let it out through your nose. When you breathe out through your nose, it gets the air right to your amygdala to put out that fire.

Sometimes—like when your mom or dad is having a birthday— there are a whole lot of candles on that cake, and sometimes

*in your brain there's a lot going on and there's a really big fire, so
big you might not be able to put it all out in just three breaths. So
you can just keep taking deep breaths until you feel more calm and
relaxed, and then you know the fire is out.*

Bringing awareness to the breath is just one of the tools I use
to combat the stress response; we'll get into many of the others
later in the book when we talk about mindfulness. But for now,
just know that this exercise can help kids feel they have some control over these "out-of-control" emotions and some tools to use
when they're feeling upset. Just as it's comforting for parents to
realize, "Hey, there's a reason I feel this way, and there's something I can do to make it better," it can be comforting for children of all ages to feel the same. Whether it helps them get over
not being picked for a team or allows them to calm themselves
before the SATs, these tools help kids take more control over
their lives and their reactions. As a parent, you will notice a difference as your child goes from being amygdala-centered to being able to access the "smart" part of her brain.

The Effects of the Breath

It's amazing, and true, that breathing can offer us that much relief
from our stress response and give us back some control over our reactions. Look at what we are able to effect in our own bodies when
we use a calming or mindfulness exercise involving the breath:

+ Your core temperature goes up; your hands and feet feel
   warm.
+ Your breathing and heart rate slow.

+ You balance the production of neurotransmitters such as do-pamine, serotonin, and norepinephrine, producing a relaxed yet alert state of mind.
+ You are better able to focus and concentrate.
+ You react thoughtfully rather than impulsively.
+ You think more clearly.
+ You solve problems effectively.
+ You experience more positive emotions.
+ You experience greater feelings of empathy.
+ You are able to access the prefrontal cortex, or the thinking and rational parts, of your brain.

In addition to breathing as a self-calming exercise, the following chapters in this book offer scores of concrete tips, suggestions, and techniques to help you either eliminate stressors from yours and your family's life or manage the stress you do experience more elegantly, thus lowering your overall stress level. We might have been born into Generation Stress, but this doesn't mean we have to be defined by it. If you learn one lesson from reading this book I hope it's that our brain is hardwired to function in certain ways but is ultimately *highly adaptable*. If we change our behavior, our brain will follow.

PART II

Simplify: Finding and Eliminating Hidden Stressors

THREE

(Over)Stimulated

A year or so ago I was asked to give a talk entitled "Creating Peaceful Homes." As part of my presentations to parents, I often include a discussion of our overstimulated, plugged-in kids and the effects of technology on our lives. What I describe as outcomes of overstimulation sounds familiar to a lot of parents. I talk about kids with short attention spans, kids who have difficulty staying on task, or older kids who never seem truly present. I'll never forget the mother who approached me after that talk on "Creating Peaceful Homes." She'd really enjoyed the talk, she told me, especially because she was at her wit's end as a parent. She expressed her complete exasperation with her inattentive teenager. "I don't know what her problem is. She just won't pay attention!" the mother complained, all the while pecking at the tiny screen she held in front of her face. I couldn't tell you the color of her eyes, because she never once looked up from her smartphone while talking to me.

There are signs all around us that times have indeed changed. There was a period when the term *24/7 parenting* meant you had a young baby at home and so were up around the clock! The early days of parenthood are long and exhausting, but it's a finite period, a phase to pass through so you can get back to normal. Well, now *24/7 parenting* means something different. Our new normal. We fill every minute of every day with texting, talking, IM'ing, blogging, updating our status on Facebook, sending e-mails to clients in different time zones, and streaming videos on our computers. Even if we're reading, increasingly the chances are we're reading on a screen. Families today are so attached to their gadgets that you'll sometimes find people texting each other from across the room. It becomes nearly impossible to be truly present anywhere, when our gadgets have our minds constantly linked to a person or event somewhere else. This is a major obstacle to leading a mindful life.

Don't get me wrong. I'm no Luddite. I've got a smartphone and a laptop, and yes, I even watch TV. I love using technology to Skype with my family on both coasts. So I'm not going to use this chapter to argue that we should all throw our computers out the window. In fact, I believe that technology can be put to wonderful use. It can help connect us across great distances, give us increased access to information, and allow working parents to adjust our schedules so as to be more available to our kids. A working mom can catch her daughter's soccer game during the day *and* catch up on e-mails after the kids go to bed. Curricula available on tablet computers means kids don't have to drag textbooks around in a suitcase. Students can study art exhibits at museums all over the world, thanks to online collections. Teachers are available for e-mailing with parents, allowing for more quick check-ins and better dialogue.

The key is in managing technology rather than letting technology manage us. Currently we don't trade our work outside the office for downtime; we simply use technology to work more, and have traded in downtime altogether. And increasingly, we're not only using technology all the time, we're using it all at the *same* time. As mentioned in chapter one, research shows that on an average day, "media multitasking" allows kids to pack a total of ten hours and forty-five minutes' worth of media into seven and a half hours. Kids use computers for schoolwork, to update their Facebook status, and to watch TV—all while texting on their phones. Aside from the social and psychological effects of our interacting with screens instead of with one another, there are the physiological effects. Developmentally, we are seeing reduced opportunities to develop empathy, a critical part of our stress management system. And with all this stimulating activity we see increased fight, flight, or freeze action in the brain, with the full stress response that comes with it.

What's Happening in the Brain

You'll remember from the last chapter that we develop empathy through face-to-face interactions, beginning as infants. It's how we learn to relate to one another, decode signals about how others are feeling, and respond to those feelings. Face-to-face interactions are the basis for our communication and relationships with others. However, as we increasingly hide behind screens, the opportunity to develop empathy is lost. Take even seemingly benign actions such as a mom breastfeeding her baby with her computer or phone next to her. While texting with friends can support isolated moms, and staying connected to work via e-mail may even increase the amount of time a mom can stay home with her child, it also means Mom is looking at the screen rather than into her baby's eyes, which is how a baby first learns to react and respond to other humans. Parents are now more apt to be talking on the phone instead of to their kids as they stroll through the park together or visit the playground. Our increased isolation, even within our own families, is affecting how we develop the skills we need to relate meaningfully to one another.

Apart from altering our development of empathy, we can't forget the effect of technology on our old friend the amygdala. As we learned in the last chapter, when stressed, our body plays out a very specific and predictable sequence of events designed to prepare us for the worst and keep us from harm. Though we think of many technology-based pastimes, such as watching TV or playing video games, as "downtime," from a neurological perspective they are anything but. This is true not just for us as adults, but even more so for our kids.

Let's take a look at what's going on behind the scenes when our kids are engaged with technology.

TELEVISION

One of the major, overlooked causes of the stress response is the simple act of watching television. With its quick pacing, flashing images, changing camera angles, and sudden, loud noises all crammed into twenty-three minutes plus commercials, TV creates havoc in our brains.

When we're watching television, our prefrontal cortex (the area of the brain that's mostly in charge of learning, empathy, and concentration) sits idly by, while the amygdala is highly alert, trying to figure out what's happening with all the quick images and to formulate a response.

SpongeBob *versus* Mister Rogers

Before *SpongeBob* or *Ben 10* arrived on the scene, children's programming was defined by such classics as *Mister Rogers' Neighborhood,* whose pacing and tone now seem nearly archaic. In each episode, Mister Rogers would greet his audience and, while singing them a little song, slowly take off his sport coat and hang it up in the closet, then remove his shoes and put on a pair of Keds—adhering to a simple routine and taking his time. Kids could process this information and easily follow the story line. They had time to consider Fred Rogers's words and wonder what adventure he would take them on that day. He was approachable and nice; a soothing character.

Now I want you to try a little experiment that's easy to do, thanks to YouTube—see, technology isn't *all* bad. Search for the introduction of *Mister Rogers' Neighborhood,* watch it, and then watch the intro for *SpongeBob SquarePants.*

When I show these clips during parenting seminars, the reactions can be telling. One mom admitted to me that as soon as she saw a few seconds of the *Mister Rogers' Neighborhood* clip, she wanted me to move on. *Okay, I get it,* she thought. *It's Mister Rogers. What's next?*

That's just the problem: We're living in such a "What's next?" world that anything less than instant gratification is unacceptable. Thanks to TiVo and DVR, we have at our fingertips every show we want. No commercials, no waiting—just skip to the good parts. No need to anticipate or *think* about what's to come. In addition, we are no longer able to focus on one thing at a time, no longer able to give things our complete attention. Our heightened state of stress is somewhat responsible for that, but a large part of the blame for our inability to focus lies with television and

media in general. From a young age, we are conditioned to expect constant stimulation and frequent payoffs. And just like lab
rats, we adjust to our conditioning.

One of the slightly more sinister aspects of kids' cartoons today is that the programming is created using principles first developed by advertisers—techniques that give your brain no choice
but to pay attention. In an article that appeared in *AAP News* in
1998 (a publication of the American Academy of Pediatrics), Dr.
Jane M. Healy writes that advertisers learned that if you flashed
images across the screen rapidly, it captured people's brains invol-
untarily. Kids are nearly held captive to such flashing images, not
to mention sounds and rapidly cycling characters and narratives;
their brains just fire away, piqued by the amygdala's desire to figure out *What's going on? What am I seeing? Is this threatening? Is it
exciting? Should I be on alert right now?*

So we sit there mesmerized, looking like we're just lazily
lounging on the couch when all the while our stress centers are
getting an exhausting workout trying to interpret the images pa-
rading in front of our eyes. And with repeat exposure, those neural pathways from the thalamus to the amygdala, those pathways
leading to the stress response, rapidly become the paths of least
resistance.

A group of four-year-old children were the subjects of a study
published in the medical journal *Pediatrics* in September 2011.
The sixty children were randomly assigned into three groups: One
group watched *SpongeBob SquarePants,* the second group watched
the slower-paced cartoon *Caillou,* and the third group was told to
draw. The children watched TV or drew for just nine minutes,
and then they took mental function tests. Now, despite whether
you find Caillou as insufferable a character as I do, there's no arguing that the pace and tone of the show is better for the brain

than those shows crammed with noises, shouting, yelling, color, and fast-moving montages. In the study, the kids who watched *SpongeBob* did significantly worse on the tests than the other two groups.

The study shows that even just very short-term exposure to this kind of television can cause measurable learning deficits. Common sense tells us that more exposure is likely to cause longer-lasting problems. Scientifically, we know that the camera cuts and loud sounds on television trigger (and are meant to trigger) what is called the "orienting response," the brain reflex that tells us there has been a change in the environment. But remember, your brain wants you focused on the task at hand if you're experiencing potential danger, even if that danger is just Squidward yelling at SpongeBob. When we experience the orienting response, our gamma brain waves—the brain waves that help us focus—essentially flatline. Because kids are still building those neural pathways, the more television they watch, the harder it becomes for them to maintain focus and attention.

PHONES, E-MAILS, AND TEXT MESSAGES

Now add in all the other gadgets that cause activation of the fight, flight, or freeze response. Every time a phone rings, it can cause the amygdala to activate. Every time a text message or e-mail arrives—*bing!*—you're forced to interpret the emotions and motivations of the sender without hearing a voice or being able to read body language for context. *Did she mean that as an insult?* you wonder. Texted smiley faces and LOLs go only so far; with more than 90 percent of our communication occurring nonverbally, misinterpretation is rampant, as communication skills are significantly impaired when we lose the visual cues. This is difficult

But My Child Is Already a TV Addict! What Do I Do?

If your child is already watching more television than you would like, the process of reducing or eliminating TV time can be intimidating, but it's not impossible. Before tackling your kid's TV habits, it is important to reflect honestly on your part in his TV watching. Often kids who watch a lot of TV have parents who watch a lot. So you'll need to cut down on your own TV viewing. Think of it as a new, better way to interact with your kids. You will also want to think about the timing of the change. Eliminating TV when someone is sick can make the reduction process more difficult. Plan in advance and embrace the challenge! Here are a few ideas to help you cut the cord, quite literally. Pick one or two that will work for you and your family.

* **Cancel Cable.** This is drastic, but obviously effective. Tell your kids in advance that you are getting rid of the cable or dish or whatever you have. You can explain to them that TV is not good for their brains and that, as a family, you are all going to take a break from it. If you are able, take the money that would normally be spent on the cable bill and spend it on arts and crafts supplies, board games, puzzles, and other brain-building forms of entertainment. You can also save it and put it toward a family vacation the kids can help plan. The hundred dollars a month or more you will save can add up quite quickly for a nice family trip!
* **Do a Cleanse.** Take a total break from the TV and other problematic electronics for a week and see what emerges. Call it Pioneer Week or another clever name. Also, ask your kids if there are things about *your* technology use that bother them. Perhaps they don't like it when you respond to e-mails while

at the breakfast table, or that you send texts at their soccer games. Make a commitment as a family to eliminate, for a set amount of time, any technology that is not related to work or school. You can then be more intentional about how you reintroduce it into your family's routine.

* **Buy Help.** Purchase a system such as BOB or the Time Machine, to control access to TV channels and enforce time limits. (Each is available at electronics stores or online.) You can assign time limits for each member of the family. When his time is up, he can argue with BOB instead of you!

* **Change Screens.** Exchange the TV screen for a better one: Get your child a Kindle or another e-reader and have her read instead.

* **Get a Live Friend.** If your child is using television as an electronic pal or is lacking a playmate, allow friends to come over if there is no sibling to entertain him. For younger kids, arrange for playdates, with no TV as one of the rules.

* **Read the Book.** Trade TV for reading a book from which a film was made, and then watch the movie based on the book. You can have fun comparing the differences between the two and talking about why the filmmakers made changes to the story or how you'd recast the movie if you were in charge. The rule is your kids must finish the book before they can watch the movie.

* **Watch Movies Only.** Switch to a movie-only model—no TV series or shows. Check out movies from the library or rent them old-school instead of downloading them, to erase the instant-gratification model. Pick movies that you will enjoy watching as a family.

* **Make Technology New Again.** Enroll your kids in a class to learn computer animation, music production, or moviemaking, so that they can engage in different types of screen time at home.

enough for us when we read an e-mail sent by a co-worker. Imagine how bewildering it is for a teen or tween whose entire social life is enacted through technology.

I recently interviewed teens about their cell phone use and found that as much as they love those phones, they are still conflicted. One seventeen-year-old girl remarked, "There are times when I will text my friends and tell them I am really struggling and they will text me back with a 'cheer up' or a 'feel better' with a smiley face. What I really need from them is a hug, and I just can't get it."

This is why some people absolutely hate talking on the phone, even if they don't consciously realize this is the reason. Without visual cues, it can be very hard to know if the person on the other end is rolling his eyes while you're talking, getting bored by what you're saying, or smiling and nodding in rapt attention. And this uncertainty in human interaction is stressful.

VIDEO GAMES

Once upon a time, if we wanted to play a video game we made a trip to the arcade. In 1996 the U.S. entertainment software industry sold 74 million units (games and consoles) to customers. Fifteen years later, that number had jumped to 246 million units, with sales predicted to continue rising. Between consoles and computers, video games are here to stay.

Let's take a trip inside your child's head while he is playing. We won't even choose a blatantly violent game, but rather, a more "benign" one, such as *Super Mario Bros.*

What is your child trying to accomplish in this game? He has to stomp on angry mushrooms and kick turtles around, dodge man-eating plants, avoid falling down deep holes, elude giant bullets, not fall into a lava pit, not drown, not get stung by a jelly-fish, not get hit by a random fireball, and save the princess before the timer runs out.

In short, death is around every corner, and your child is sup-posed to keep up this frantic pace for an extended amount of time in a life-or-death battle to save an innocent victim, all to the tune of "cheerful" carnival music on a loop. Again, this is a *benign* video game.

The amygdala is simply not good at differentiating between real-life danger and imaginary danger. So your child is in fight, flight, or freeze mode the entire time he's playing this game. It may not look as extreme as when he calls you into his room because he's sure there's a monster in his closet, but it's still an activation of the same stress-response mechanism. The more he plays, the more es-tablished those neural pathways become—and the effects are cu-mulative. The results could take the form of a weakened attention span and impulse control, or even more aggressive behavior.

Kids now play video games not only while sitting in front of the television, of course, but also on an array of hand-held devices, on the computer, and even on theirs or their parents' cell phones or tablet computers. It's not at all unusual to see kids sitting in res-taurants with their families with their faces buried in their gadgets while waiting for the food to arrive, or using their gadgets in the backseat of the family car, or at the dinner (or breakfast or lunch) table, or in a doctor's waiting room, or . . . pretty much anywhere.

I can't tell you how many parents of children with ADHD will say to me, "But he can focus just fine on his video games." Of course he can. Video games are all about leaving the prefrontal cor-tex alone. From *Super Mario Bros.* to *Grand Theft Auto,* video games activate the fight, flight, or freeze response. The child with ADHD doesn't need to engage the prefrontal cortex, or thinking center, in this situation, a task that is extremely difficult for someone with this condition in the best of circumstances. Playing video games fits the natural brain patterns of a child with ADHD, which are very different from the patterns used sitting in a classroom trying to listen to a teacher explain a new concept.

Media Multitasking

As I've alluded to, one of the biggest issues regarding screen time (playing video games, watching TV, texting, surfing the Internet) is that your child is engaged in not just one of these activities but many, and often all at the same time. The Kaiser Family Foundation has studied media usage among kids ages eight to eighteen. In 2010 it announced that media usage and media multitasking among that age group was way up from its previous study in 2004. According to Kaiser's results, kids in that age bracket spend seven hours and thirty-eight minutes per day using entertainment media outside the classroom—more than fifty-three hours per week. And because they do so much media multitasking (watching TV while texting, for example), they manage to pack ten hours and forty-five minutes' worth of media into those seven hours and thirty-eight minutes.

That is an hour and seventeen minutes more per day than in 2004. What's behind this increase are mostly cell phones and mp3 devices—66 percent of kids in that age group now own a cell phone (as compared to 39 percent in the earlier study), and 76 percent now own iPods or other mp3 players (as compared to 18 percent earlier).

The one piece of that puzzle that's not so alarming is the music component: Depending on the type, music can actually

enhance concentration and be calming, so it's not always triggering the fight, flight, or freeze response. But the rest of those hours?
From a neurological perspective, it's a disaster—the prefrontal
cortex is just sitting idle while the amygdala is getting stimulated
over and over again. From media alone, our kids spend between
fifty-three and seventy-five hours a week in a state of fight, flight,
or freeze.

There is good news to be had, though. Just because this is
what your kids are doing now doesn't mean you can't have more
control over how much they engage in technology. But before I
get to the suggestions for how to help, let's take a look at our own
behavior. The first place any of us needs to start in changing how
our families use technology is in being cognizant of and changing
how *we* use technology. Every time we talk on the phone while
we're taking the kids to school, mumble a response to our child
while answering an e-mail, or use the TV as background noise
while hanging around the house, we're not only wreaking havoc
on our brains from that constant use and multitasking, but we're
also modeling bad behavior for our kids.

Hanging Up and Hanging Out

In the town where I live we performed a really simple but amazing experiment. It was prompted by my husband being called out
by our kids on how much he was using his phone when he should
have been paying attention to them. My daughter bet him that he
couldn't go a week without using his phone when he was around
the kids. We all agreed that he would have to pay each child fifty
cents each time he was caught on the phone around them. After a
week, I can tell you they had enough to buy themselves a treat,

and we were stunned to learn how much time we parents spent on our phones.

So we embarked on a challenge we called Hang Up and Hang Out. Partnering with the local schools, we issued a challenge for parents to put down their cell phones in the presence of their kids for one week. This was a mild sort of technology cleanse, geared toward paying attention to the most important (little) people in our lives. When you go on a food cleanse, the goal is not to rid yourself of solid food forever, but to take a break and then be more intentional about what you put in your body. Our goal for Hang Up and Hang Out was similar: to become more intentional about how we used our phones when we resumed normal life, and to see what happened when we weren't on our phones. Would we sing along to the radio? Talk to our kids about their friends?

To kick off the challenge, kids wrote letters to their parents about why they wanted them to participate. Those letters were heartbreakingly honest. Many of them sounded like this one, from ten-year-old Ryan:

> *Dear Mom,*
>
> *Hang Up and Hang Out. I would like you to spend more time with me instead of talking on the phone with your friends. You sometimes talk at dinnertime. You also talk in the car on the way to school. And sometimes when we are having family game night. Can you try not to talk on the phone when we are having a big discussion that is very important? And sometimes when you pick me up at school you are talking on the phone with your friends. When I used to play soccer you were talking on the phone when I scored a goal. Some of the time you did not see me score for*

my team. When we are home you are talking to grandma or Gretchen. I do not mean to be rude but you need to hang up and hang out for a week or two.

Love,
Ryan

As you might have guessed, we were confronted with a lot of angry parents who were super ticked off that we were imposing this restriction on their lives, parents who said the challenge was a good idea but not for them. "I'm a real estate agent, so I *have* to use my phone . . . ," etc. Many others were inspired but didn't know where to begin. On day two of the challenge we hosted a family fun night that featured different stations teaching families how to engage without technology. There was family yoga, dinner games; we decorated boxes meant to corral and contain gadgets during meal times, and even organized a family dance party! People changed stations every ten minutes and did the rounds.

We'd had no idea what to expect when we decided to host the event, but we had 480 people show up. We were blown away. This is a clear indicator that what we were embarking on with Hang Up and Hang Out was needed by both kids and parents. Sometimes kids need to be directed and told what is good for them, and sometimes parents need to take a step back and make sure our own behavior reflects our values. The end result is worth it.

Hang Up and Hang Out took place in our town over a year ago. Last week I was approached by a mom who told me that, a year later, every time the phone rings while she is in the car or playing with her kids, she thinks about the challenge and asks

> ## What Is Hang Up and Hang Out?
>
> * A challenge to parents to curtail their cell phone use in the presence of their kids for one week.
> * An opportunity to build stronger relationships among family members.
> * A recognition that in today's time-pressed, technology-driven world, it can be challenging to find the time to stop and have meaningful engagement with those we care about most.
> * An example of how little changes make big differences.

herself if she really needs to answer the call. She said the challenge profoundly changed her interactions with her kids. It was one small change that made a big difference!

Learning to manage technology, rather than letting technology manage us, helps create an environment where families can be present in their day-to-day lives—to live more mindful lives. It is not formal mindfulness practice (which we discuss in great detail in chapter 7), but helps us create a home environment where mindful living can occur.

Solutions: Managing Technology

Now that we've got you thinking about your own technology use, here are some developmentally appropriate tools for helping your kids manage technology effectively and cool those brains down.

Early Childhood (ages 0–5)

If you are the parent of a young child, this is when modeling is really critical. Your child is watching you *every moment,* so be mindful of the indirect messages your technology use is sending her. To that end:

- Avoid using your phone or screens in the car, at the dinner table, during pickup or drop-off, or while watching your child's performance/game.
- Remember that kids can understand what it being said long before they can speak. You may not think they are paying attention, but they are. This is a great reason to avoid ambient TV in the house.
- Keep kids from TV and computer screens for as long as you can. Try to keep them engaged with low-tech toys instead: musical instruments (or spoons and pots and pans), drawing materials, building toys, books. Or keep an "everything" bin for the preschool set, into which scraps of fabric, buttons, recyclable containers, pipe cleaners, and all manner of building materials can go. You'll be amazed at what your kids create.
- When your kids do watch TV (even on your phone), follow the American Academy of Pediatrics recommendations concerning screen time. Kids under two years old should not watch *any* TV. While the AAP says that kids older than two should watch no more than one to two hours of quality programming a day, I beg to differ. In my opinion, kids this age should still watch no more than a half hour a day.
- Have them watch good stuff. Preschoolers can get help learning the alphabet through shows like *Sesame Street.* Wildlife and

nature shows are educational and exciting to watch for small kids.

- Give TV a run for its money. Go the thrift store and buy a box-ful of spangle-y dresses, capes, hats, belts, and other costume-worthy dress-up clothes. Add to it your kids' old Halloween costumes and you have a ready-made dress-up box.

Elementary (ages 5–10)

- Keep those rules for screen time in full force. Although the AAP says kids this age can watch one or two hours a day, I still recommend no more than a half hour a day for this age group. You can add a little more time on weekends.
- Avoid keeping video games in your house, even if your kids are able to play them at friends' houses. If you must have video games, choose active games, where kids dance, play instruments, play tennis, or engage in any activity that at least has them exercising while playing.
- Instead of having your kids play games on your tablet computer in the car, how about letting them listen to an audiobook? Or have them help you choose music they like and load their playlists to listen to during car trips. Music is great for the brain, reducing levels of cortisol, a stress hormone.
- Kids love to create. Keep an on-the-go art kit with you, upping the sophistication level of the types of paper and implements your kids are allowed to use. Take a portable box of LEGOs to restaurants or appointments, or have your kids play a simple travel game in the car if you'll be driving a long distance.
- Turn your recycling bin into the "invention box." Get out the glue.

- Turn off the TV and have a family dance party. Research shows that in addition to providing exercise and being a whole lot of fun, putting a little jig in your step actually reduces stress hormone levels. And turn the reins over to the kids by asking them what artist or playlist they want to hear. Then crank the music up and get out on the floor with them. But remember, this is not a time to start checking your BlackBerry. It's all about engagement and laughter, and boogeying to the beat!

- Choose your apps wisely. If your kids are going to play with your phone or tablet computer, pick games that have some educational value. Look for those that inspire creativity (art apps) or help kids learn basic academic skills. Don't make the mistake of believing you're giving your child a leg up in doing so, however. Creative play will boost your kid's learning more than playing an electronic math game.

- If your kids are going to watch TV, watch with them. Look for teachable moments in the shows. Many shows for this age group explore themes related to bullying, intimate relationships, or problems with parents. Look for opportunities to ask your child, "What would you do in this situation?"

Tweens (ages 10–13)

- You'd better believe your modeling is still in full effect with tweens. If you're talking on the phone while driving, or texting at every red light, you're glimpsing the future for that impressionable tween sitting in the backseat.

- If your tween uses computers, make sure those computers are located in a central room and not in his bedroom. Use monitoring software such as Net Nanny (www.NetNanny.com), which controls sites your kids can access.

- Keep the cell phone chargers in a central location, where cell phones should spend the night. Or keep your kids' phones in your bedroom, not theirs.
- Be aware of and limit ambient TV.
- For tweens who are into TV, use it as an opportunity to interact and do something fun together. This builds a routine that hopefully lasts through their teen years. My daughter, for example, loves *Ellen,* and we made a habit of watching it together. Look for shows that reflect your values or at least make you laugh. Laughing is a great antidote to stress, flooding your body with pleasure hormones.
- As with younger kids, look for opportunities to approach difficult topics with your tween. Some parents find it uncomfortable to talk about sexuality or drugs and alcohol with their kids. If one of these topics comes up during a show or movie, ask your kids how they feel about it. The earlier you begin having tough conversations with your child, the more likely she will be to come to you when she needs advice regarding a difficult situation.
- Be the house where your tweens and their friends want to hang out. Make them feel welcome, prepare them snacks, invite them over for movie night. This keeps you in your tweens' life and also provides some opportunity for that face time we don't get enough of.

Teens (ages 13–18)

For teenagers, most of us think of the biggest challenge is ensuring appropriate use of the phone rather than television. Just try to pry that thing out of a teenager's hand! Especially now that phones have become mini-computers, staying "connected" via phone has become a lifeline for many teens.

Lots of parents use technology as a punishment for or consequence of bad behavior, because it's a meaningful one: They get their kid's attention by taking away the phone or limiting computer time. However, try to remember that with adolescents, you are most in control as a co-pilot, helping them navigate technology's use and facilitating their ability to figure it out, rather than taking an all-or-nothing approach. My sister Lisa, a family therapist, says the teens she works with actually think of the phone as a person; it's *that* critical to them. With this in mind, why not take that line of thinking to its logical extreme?

- Talk with your teen about using the same rules with the phone that you do with friends. You can even *name* the phone if that helps make it fun—for example, let's call your teen's phone Thelma. When is it not appropriate to pay attention only to Thelma? Well, at the dinner table one wouldn't ignore all the other people seated there just to talk to Thelma. You wouldn't ignore Grandma when she's over for a visit just because Thelma was hanging out, too. Thelma might even need to go home while Grandma's over. Your teen wouldn't be allowed to talk to Thelma all night, and Thelma couldn't spend the night on a Tuesday.
- Watch for signs that your teen is not managing her phone appropriately and needs help: texting while driving, suffering sleep deprivation from texting or talking too long at night, not participating in family engagements, not attending to what's present, or feeling like the phone is a social pressure she cannot bear (having to answer a billion texts, having to update

her status constantly)—all these are good reasons to monitor your teen's cell phone use.

- Be mindful that there are gender differences around using the phone. Girls tend to use the phone as an extension of their social life. (Phone equals relationship.) Boys tend to use the phone as a means to make plans. Pay attention to these nuances so that if your teen's phone use changes, you can use the change an opportunity to engage in meaningful conversation about what's going on in his life. (For example, if texting increases dramatically, chances are your child is involved in a new relationship.)

- Help your teen understand that anything she e-mails or texts to a friend could end up becoming public. It can help your teen avoid puzzling or agonizing over whether to send a message she feels unsure about (or having to decode the message she gets back) if you break her of the illusion that the Internet and texts are private communication. Easy rule of thumb: "Would you send that text or e-mail to the whole school? No? Then say it in person."

- Teach your teens to compartmentalize. Help them to make good decisions around doing one thing at a time, avoiding multitasking. A chief operating officer of a major business headquartered in New York recently told me that he has a timer on his desk set for thirty-minute increments. He allows himself to check his e-mail only when the alarm goes off. This allows him to shut off his brain from that responsibility and focus on other tasks while knowing he will still stay connected at appropriate times, eliminating the drain of multitasking. If you know your kids are going to try to text and e-mail while they're researching a paper for school, don't tell them they have to wait until their homework is done to do so. Try having them

Tips and Tricks for Sports Fans of All Ages

I was watching my six-year-old son play soccer the other day. After making a goal, he ran around the field with his hands raised, pumping his fists. "Yes! Yes! That's Right!" he yelled, then sprinted to the center of the field, slid on his knees, and ripped his shirt off over his head. My jaw dropped in horror. Was this my child? Where was the sportsmanship?

Sports can be used in really great ways; my son learned how to add from sports scores. Sports programs also provide great and teachable moments to talk about sportsmanship and to focus on the process rather than the outcome, and they can be a great opportunity for bonding for the big sports fans in the family. But the truth is televised sports models the kind of in-your-face, highly competitive attitude I witnessed in my son that day on the soccer field. It doesn't matter how much you talk about how it's not all about winning if the TV is sending the opposite message in very appealing and convincing ways.

If you're going to let your kids watch sports on TV, watch with them. Better yet, record certain events, watch with your kids, and fast-forward through the commercials. Grab the popcorn and have fun.

do homework for thirty minutes, then e-mail or text for fifteen, then back to homework.

- If your teen wants to engage in technology, encourage her to interact more with music and less with e-mails and games. Have her create playlists, or even ask her to create playlists for you to use when you work out, or for a family road trip. Talk to her about the music and artists she likes and why.

FOUR

(Over)Scheduled

A friend of mine was having difficulty with her young daughter, whom I'll call Eva. Eva was a typical, happy-go-lucky kid until about the middle of first-grade. It was then, her mom confided, that she suddenly became anxious and defiant. Tantrums were common. She refused to eat nearly everything, and meals became a battle of wills. Bedtime, likewise, was a nightmare. Eva just couldn't and wouldn't settle down. There was nothing easy for her or about her anymore. Looking back to her kindergarten self, her parents were bewildered, frustrated, and upset. What in the world had changed? Was there anything they could do?

After a lengthy conversation, I suggested to Eva's mother that she write out a schedule that showed what her daughter did each day. Once she did that, I told her to color the stimulating activities in red and the calming activities or downtime in blue. (Keep in mind that we've just learned that television is stimulating, not calming. We'll learn more in the next chapter that "leisure" activities that are adult-led and that involve kids' following rules are also stimulating. Unstructured playtime would be included as downtime).

Here's what Eva's schedule looked like:

Monday	Tuesday	Wednesday	Thursday	Friday
6:30–7:30am Wake up/ Get ready	6:30–7:30am Wake up/ Get ready	6:30–7:30am Wake up/ Get ready	6:30–7:30am Wake up/ Get ready	6:30–7:30am Wake up/ Get ready
7:30–8:15am Bus	7:30–8:15am Bus	7:30–8:15am Bus	7:30–8:15am Bus	7:30–8:15am Bus
8:30–3:15am School	8:30–3:15am School	8:30–3:15am School	8:30–3:15am School	8:30–3:15am School
3:15–4pm Snack	3:15–4pm Snack	3:15–4pm Snack	3:15–4pm Snack	3:15–4pm Snack
4–5pm Soccer	4–5pm Gymnastics	4–5pm Soccer	4–5pm Gymnastics	4–5pm Play Date
5–5:30pm Drive Home	5–5:30pm Drive Home	5–5:30pm Drive Home	5–5:30pm Drive Home	5–5:30pm Drive Home
5:30–6pm TV	5:30–6pm TV	5:30–6pm TV	5:30–6pm TV	5:30–6pm TV
6–7pm Homework	6–7pm Homework	6–7pm Homework	6–7pm Homework	6–7pm Homework
7–7:30pm Dinner	7–7:30pm Dinner	7–7:30pm Dinner	7–7:30pm Dinner	7–7:30pm Dinner
7:30–8pm Practice Piano	7:30–8pm Practice Piano	7:30–8pm Practice Piano	7:30–8pm Practice Piano	7:30–8pm Practice Piano
8–9pm Bath, Read, Bed	8–9pm Bath, Read, Bed	8–9pm Bath, Read, Bed	8–9pm Bath, Read, Bed	8–9pm Bath, Read, Bed

Notice that on most days Eva had only one and a half hours of calming activities or downtime during the entire day: dinner, bath time, and reading before bed. Because of the pressures of standardized testing, many schools are cutting out or cutting back on recess and any other free time, meaning that the vast majority of the school day is stimulating, with almost no breaks for unstructured activities. Also notice that Eva awoke at 6:30 A.M. each day and went to bed at 9:00 P.M., which means she wasn't getting enough sleep. That's nine and a half hours (if she fell asleep immediately), while the National Sleep Foundation recommends she get ten to eleven.

Eva had after-school activities four out of five weekdays, plus she practiced piano every day. That left just one hour per weekday of unstructured playtime with a friend. She went from stimulating activity to stimulating activity without any time for jumping rope or doodling or pretending she was a ninja princess. She didn't even gaze idly out the window in transport. While she was in the car between activities, she'd eat a snack while watching a DVD.

Now, I don't know what you did in first grade, but I did not share Eva's schedule. After school I went home, had a snack, and played with my friends outside until dinner. Eva's life, by contrast, was already, by the age of six, as hectic as that of a Manhattan magazine mogul. What's more troubling, however, is that her schedule *is not unusual.*

I know a lot of parents who are crazed just trying to keep up with their kids' schedules. They are always either driving somewhere or attending a game or locating a track uniform (or ballet shoes), all while falling behind on outside work or housework, or both. Just writing this description makes me feel a little anxious, as if *I* were in the midst of this rat race. A schedule that frenzied feels bad to parents and it feels just as bad to kids—only children don't have the wherewithal to say, "Hey, Mom? I'm feeling like my plate's a little full. Could I cut back on the after-school activities a bit?" They just show symptoms of stress: They whine and argue; they become picky eaters; they refuse to go to bed; and then they toss and turn when they get there. And as parents we don't dare put the brakes on, because we feel we'll let little Jimmy down if he isn't a bilingual black belt by the second grade. The message modern society sends us is clear: If we're not providing enough "enrichment" or extracurricular activities, even in early childhood, our kids will get left behind.

It's not just our afternoons that are crazed. When was the last time you talked to a parent who loved getting kids ready for school in the morning? Mornings are often a frenzy of activity, with parents screaming at their kids to hurry up and get dressed, kids running around like maniacs trying to find their shoes or books or homework, and everyone checking e-mail on their phones as they walk out the door. The kids might eat in the car on the way to school while you grab a coffee and prepare to do battle with traffic. Does this sound at all familiar to you? If you could, would you want it to change?

What's Happening in the Brain

It will probably come as no surprise that leading lives this hectic means subjecting your brain and your children's brains to near-constant stimulation. After a busy, frenetic morning, both you and your children arrive at your destinations with brains on high alert and in a state of stress. You already know you're not at your best when you walk into your office after a stressful morning. What you might not realize is that how your child begins her day makes a huge impact on how long it will take until she's settled down and ready to learn, and on what and how much she can absorb at school. Even many teachers don't recognize that their students arrive in many different states of mind. Teachers often lack the necessary tools to help calm and center students before beginning the day's lessons. And once school lets out, we're back to high alert, trying to feed our kids a quick snack while getting them to start their homework, all before rushing back out of the house to head to ballet or soccer or piano lessons. And with every game and lesson we rush off to, and with every news report we hear and phone call we answer along the way, we are reinforcing the stress response.

These hectic schedules become a significant hindrance to our ability to create mindful lives. We enter a constant mode of planning and spend little to no time just *being*. We're planning the kids' schedules, organizing carpools, racing to make it to our destination on time. When we arrive our minds shift directly to thinking about the next event, rarely enjoying exactly where we are. Kids naturally live in the present moment, but we are increasingly denying them this opportunity, at younger and younger ages. To truly enjoy the present moment we have to allow ourselves and our kids time to just *be*.

Buried Under Homework

For parents of kids starting elementary school, one of the primary reasons their kids are overscheduled is because of a burgeoning load of homework. For reasons that include pressures to meet state standards and increase standardized test scores, and the belief that work out of school increases a child's chances of getting into a good college, today's children face more hours of daily homework than ever before. Yet increasingly studies show that assigning mountains of homework doesn't make our kids smarter or better learners or land them guaranteed spots at Harvard. In fact, excess homework stresses them out, keeps them from important developmental practices such as creative play, unstructured games, and community engagement; and takes a toll on their diet and sleep habits.

After attending Back-to-School Night at her son's private high school, a friend called me in a state of panic. Jaden, her sixteen-year-old son, is a very bright junior and a strong athlete who plays varsity football and baseball at this athletic powerhouse of a school. That year, he would be taking a full load of honors and AP courses. During Back-to-School Night his mom spent ten minutes in each of his classes. Teacher after teacher told the parents that "*this* course" would be the most difficult class their child would ever take and that they should expect a couple of hours of homework each night. Consequently, the parents should not be surprised when their son or daughter came to them wanting to drop the class. My friend left the school that evening on the verge of a panic attack, and she wasn't even the one taking the classes! Her son already arrived home each night no earlier than seven o'clock due to practices and games. If they ate dinner together he wouldn't be able to start his homework until 7:30. He had a total of five courses, and in each he could expect two hours of homework a night. I'm no mathematician, but how is that supposed to work?

In 2012 the Race to Nowhere community (the group that created a remarkable documentary on the pressures that our high-schoolers face) and Change.org petitioned the National PTA to adopt homework guidelines that take these excessive homework demands into account. In part, they based their request on scientific research such as Duke University professor Harris Cooper's 2006 survey of fifteen years' worth of homework studies. Cooper found no correlation between academic performance and homework for elementary school kids, and in fact found that middle and high school kids' academic performance suffered as the hours of homework increased beyond what the National Education Association recommended. A 2011 study in the *Economics of Education Review* found that homework in certain areas—science, English, and history—had little or no impact on the test scores received by the eighth-graders studied.

Perhaps more important, all that homework is doing a number on the stress levels of our children, leading not to intellectual curiosity but to burnout. In a 2005 study by the Lucile Packard

Homework Recommendations

If you find your child's school policies grossly out of line with the recommendations here, it might be worth starting a dialogue with your child's teacher or the school administrators.

* **Beginning in first grade, children should do no more than ten minutes per night per grade.**
* Homework is more effective when it challenges and engages students rather than depends on rote memorization or repetition.
* Homework should not be assigned over the weekend or when students are out sick or on school break.
* If your teen is buried under hours of homework each night, do some investigating. Do the other kids at school have the same issue? Is there a way to streamline homework time to make it more efficient? Communicate with your teen and, if needed, the school about your concerns.

Foundation for Children's Health, a full 70 percent of parents in the Bay Area of California reported that their nine- to thirteen-year-olds were suffering moderate to high stress levels, with homework topping the list of stressors. As we've learned in the past few chapters, a stressed brain is not a brain ready to learn or record information, so massive homework loads actually might inhibit our kids' learning. And while we're perhaps rightly worried about how much our tweens and teens text or watch YouTube, a study by Scholastic found that the number one reason children over the age of eight stopped reading for pleasure was too much homework.

So how much homework is okay? While many education advocates say we need both less homework and a different kind of homework, one not based on rote learning—do *you* remember loving those math worksheets? Neither do I—at the very least we can use the basic guidelines of ten minutes per grade per child set by the National Education Association and the National PTA. This means that seniors should be topping out at two hours maximum per night.

Make Scheduling and Routine Work for You

Do you ever wonder how child care centers can get a roomful of three-year-olds to nap at the same time? It's all about the routine. When kids don't know what to expect, it can cause feelings of anxiety, and the result is resistance. When they know what to expect, it's much easier for them to transition from one activity to the next and to stay in a peaceful state of mind.

Kids feel a sense of safety when they know that, for example, they're first going to have breakfast at the table and then brush their teeth, get dressed, read a book with Dad, kiss Mom good-bye, and get on the school bus. Getting used to this particular routine means that they'll no longer become upset that they're allowed to eat breakfast in front of the television some mornings but not allowed to on others. (As we learned in the last chapter, starting the day with TV isn't doing them any favors anyway.)

Likewise, it's good for them to have scheduled time when they get together with other kids on a regular basis for some structured activities. They have their school friends and their gymnastics or soccer friends. If they haven't made great friends in one place, they may find their "tribe" in another. And they may find activities that really get them interested and excited, thus giving them something to look forward to.

Routines are important for kids, but that doesn't mean we need to control everything they do. There's a big difference between creating a morning or dinner routine (which we'll address a bit later) and filling an after-school schedule with adult-led activities.

"UNSCHEDULE" YOUR CHILDREN

Right now I am giving you permission *not* to sign up your child for soccer and Boy Scouts and karate this year. You're not cheating him out of any important life experiences, putting him at risk for ridicule in gym class, or ruining his chances at an Olympic gold medal. There. Doesn't that feel better?

Not yet? Okay, let me convince you some more. Parents today are getting hit with carefully targeted marketing that subtly, and sometimes not so subtly, convinces us that our kids are not going to get into the right colleges, are not going to succeed in life, and are going to end up picking up cans on the side of the road if we don't sign them up for Pee Wee athletics and kindergarten readiness programs by the time they turn three. You feel guilty at the thought of not signing up your child because the messages are *designed* to cause you guilt, and anxiety, and encourage you to place your child in said activity. The fact of the matter is unscheduling your kids is one of the best things you can do for them. Ensuring that your family has plenty of downtime to engage and connect as a family, and that your kids have time for creative play to ensure healthy brain development, is a much more likely indicator of future success and happiness than enrolling them in that extra dance class.

That said, there is merit to having some structured activities in your children's lives; kids who have no structured activities tend to fare worse in school, have fewer friends, and experience less self-confidence, so I'm by no means suggesting that you pull your kids out of everything. You just want to be selective and make sure your child isn't so overscheduled that there's no time for meaningful interactions with the family, creative play, or self-directed activities.

HOW MANY DAYS A WEEK?

My recommendation is that kids under the age of eight be in structured activities no more than two days a week, and that the activities be chosen by the children when possible. Choosing the activity, however, does not give them the authority to quit the activity halfway through or attend practices only on days when they feel like it. If they make a commitment to play basketball, they need to honor that commitment and play the whole season. If, after completing the full season, they decide they want to try something else, then by all means let them give something new a shot. For older kids (around nine to twelve), it's okay to increase this to three to four days a week (including weekends). Teenagers can handle extracurricular activities three to five days a week.

THE SCHEDULE WORKSHEET

As Eva's parents found out, it can be a real eye-opener to see your child's schedule written out in worksheet form, especially when it is color-coded for stimulating activities. For younger kids, I recommend that at least two whole afternoons per week and one per weekend be left open for unstructured play—building a fort with sheets, arm-wrestling, putting on a doll fashion show, playing

	Sun.	Mon.	Tues.	Wed.	Thurs.	Fri.	Sat.
5am							
6am							
7am							
8am							
9am							
10am							
11am							
12pm							
1pm							
2pm							
3pm							
4pm							
5pm							
6pm							
7pm							
8pm							
9pm							
10pm							

Table 4.1. Your Schedule Worksheet

with friends or family, or both. For older kids, look at how much time is being taken up with schoolwork, or use the schedule to have a frank conversation about their screen time and any multitasking they're doing to keep up. Everyone's schedule (including yours) should allow for some downtime.

Now try using a colored pencil to shade in all the stimulating activities in red and all the calming activities or downtime in blue. Do you see mostly red? If so, there's a problem: There needs to be a better balance. Figure out which red activities you can turn blue.

At the beginning of each season, sit down as a family to discuss the activities that everyone would like to participate in—parents included; you need activities, too. Lay out all the options and make decisions about new activities you would like to try or those you'd like to continue, mixing up sports, arts, and character building-type programs such as Girl Scouts or religious education. Diversity of activities leads to a well-rounded child. This does not occur when we decide at age six that Johnny is going to be a soccer star. In addition to preventing potential burnout at a young age, a variety of activities exposes your child to different interests that stimulate different areas of his brain. He then develops a variety of skills, so if one thing doesn't work out, he has other skills to fall back on.

If You're Going to Schedule One Thing, Make It Dinner

Dinner should be a priority as a family, and it shouldn't involve televisions or gadgets. Ignore the phone, don't grab food and go, and don't eat in shifts. Make sure that it's not set up so that Mom and Dad talk to each other while the kids are left out of the

conversation. Don't let the kids interrupt or dominate conversation, either. Make a point of ensuring that everyone gets a turn to
talk about his day, thoughts, and feelings.

Research has shown again and again that families who eat together have better bonds. Reputable studies in peer-reviewed journals have concluded that kids who regularly eat dinner with their
families have better communication with their parents; do better in
school; believe their parents are proud of them; get fewer eating
disorders as adolescents; have better diet quality and meal planning
as young adults; eat more fruits and vegetables; are more commit-
ted to learning; feel better about themselves; and are less likely to be
depressed, drink alcohol while underage or use drugs, smoke, commit suicide, run away from home, steal, cause property damage, or
be violent. All that just from eating dinner as a family!

Make Mealtimes Fun

Even though it's your family, and even though it's "just" dinner,
you may feel a little awkward at first making dinnertime a concentrated bonding effort. How do you get everyone focused? What
do you talk about? How do you keep them at the table? Here are
some solutions that work for me.

On some nights at our dinner table, we start with a minute of
silence. This probably comes off as counterintuitive. We spend
our days waiting for dinnertime to have a family discussion, yet
we start with silence? Absolutely. From the moment we wake
up, we are *doing*. We plan, prepare, organize, and regret, but rarely
do we have the opportunity just to *be*. One minute a day just being can go a long way. And as dinnertime nears, with the culmi-
nation of the workday and after-school activities colliding into

homework and bedtime routines, we need to catch our collective breath. You will discover that a minute of silence allows you to do just that, bridging the gap between your chaotic day and your desire to have a peaceful evening.

I have an hourglass timer from a board game that the kids get to turn over at the start of dinner. While the sand trickles down from one end to the other, there's no talking. This was a challenge for my four-year-old the first time we did it. It took a few tries, but his competitive nature got the best of him, and he was so proud when that last piece of sand trickled through. During this minute, my kids are allowed to eat if they want to (and they actually get a good amount of eating done in that minute because they're not focused on anything else!). After that minute of silence, we feel centered, present, and ready to engage with one another. For older kids, the moment of silence is a great reminder of being present and helps them get used to silence in the absence of beeps, chirps, buzzes, and dings. When the minute is up, we often ask one another what we were thinking about during the minute. This makes for a good segue into creating meaningful conversation.

Too often at dinner tables, parents of young children are so obsessed with what their child has or has not eaten that the entire meal turns into one huge power struggle. There is no conversation, no exchange of feelings or ideas. The focus is on whether your daughter ate enough broccoli to warrant getting dessert. Who needs that? What about if you gave up the struggle and tried to have more fun?

I'm not saying that what they eat is not important. It certainly is. What I'm saying is if you offer your kids healthy choices and you engage them in conversation at the dinner table, they will eat. They will also be less likely to overeat or to struggle with eating disorders in the future if meals are framed in terms of connection and sharing instead of associated with power struggles and stress.

Another way to keep them at the dinner table is through dinner games. Dinner games are all about communication and family bonding. We actually have a "Mindful Life Meal Wheel" game on our dinner table (available at http://www.mindfullifetoday.com /product_p/mealwheel.htm). Each family member takes turns spinning the wheel and is then prompted to answer questions like "Who was a good friend to you today?" or "What is something you appreciate about the person to your left?" Several companies put out decks of cards with family conversation starters. Among them are Chat Pack for Kids and Table Topics Family (for families with school-age kids; available online) and Family Talk and Grandparent Talk (for ages four and up, available at www.aroundthe tablegames.com). Beginner Dinner Games (ages three to six) and Dinner Games and Activities (ages five to twelve) combine some conversation starters with simple-to-play dinner games that don't require game pieces, and they're both available online.

Dinner conversations provide a way for kids to process their feelings and open up about things they might not otherwise talk about. One of the key elements of this process is that Mom and Dad have to be willing to be honest, too—if you talk about the mistakes you made that day, your kids will realize it's okay for them to talk about those things. And if they can talk about those things in a neutral context, without getting yelled at or nagged, it'll be a lot more likely for them to really hear and process the lessons and advice they need.

I once saw an interview with Sara Blakely, the wildly successful inventor of Spanx, in which she talked about the family dinner conversations that took place while she was growing up. She said that they would go around the table, with each one talking about something he or she had done right that day and a mistake they'd made. Talking so easily about mistakes helped Blakely learn that it was okay to take risks and okay to fail sometimes; she credits those dinner conversations, in part, for helping her take the big risk of starting her own company—which, as most women know, has reached amazing heights.

In the end, it isn't about exactly what you do or what you talk about; the thing that makes dinnertime beneficial for kids and helpful for families is that you spend the time devoted to talking with one another without distractions. You can learn lots about each other and have a great time together simply by intentionally making an effort to be present at the table.

So, the next time you're feeling pressured to sign your child up for yet another activity that'll look good on a college application, remember the big picture: If your main goal is to ensure your child will have a happy and healthy life, nothing goes farther than prioritizing the family dinner. Minimize the stress and enjoy your time around the table. Those two things will have a protective effect on your child throughout life that no clarinet lesson ever could.

Solutions: Dinner Togetherness

Early Childhood and Elementary (ages 0–10)

- Rose, Bud, Thorn. At the dinner table each night, try playing Rose, Bud, Thorn with your kids. (Of all the activities I suggest when I work with parents, this is the one I get the most positive feedback about.) Your "rose" is the best thing that happened to you that day, your "bud" is something you're looking forward to the next day, and your "thorn" is something that didn't go the way you wanted it to. Everyone at the table takes a turn. Putting one's "thorns" in context like this allows kids to talk about their problems at a neutral time, discuss mistakes they made, and get family feedback on a problem without having to bring it up themselves. Young kids love playing this game, and they will continue to ask for it as they grow older.

- Mitt Mystery. Everyone in the family takes turns putting a "mystery" item in an oven mitt. Other family members reach into the mitt and try to figure out what the object is without pulling the object out. This is a fun little activity to promote family togetherness.

Elementary (ages 5–10)

- Who Was a Good Friend? Ask your child, "Who was a good friend to you today?" Kids this age can get very caught up in peers who are not so kind all the time. This question helps them focus on the qualities of good friends and may help them recognize friendships that are healthy to pursue.
- Mindful Life Meal Wheel. Try a spin on the Mindful Life Meal Wheel (http://www.mindfullifetoday.com/product_p /mealwheel.htm). Each member of the family takes a turn spinning the wheel and answering a question. Questions include "What is something you appreciate about the person to your left?" and "What mistake did you make that you learned from today?"

Tween and Teens (ages 10–18)

- With increasing activities for older kids, dinners often get eliminated. If baseball practice always runs late and games last until 8:30, family dinner will be the first thing to go. When deciding on an activity schedule, build family dinner into the schedule and make it a priority.

- For older kids who seem superbooked, make Sunday night a priority dinner. Set a nice table, break out the fancy dishes, have everyone dress up, and try to get your tween or teen to cook with you. Also, you can plan several courses that keep the family at the table for a while.

Pleasant Mornings That Work for the Whole Family

Now that dinner is under control, I'm here to tell you that your days can begin differently, too, starting tomorrow. And you don't need to move house or change jobs (or children) in order for this to happen. The smallest changes can indeed make a difference.

When my son, Charlie, was about four he would wake up and immediately become clingy, whiny, and super needy. Mornings became more and more stressful as his neediness escalated and our frustration grew. Then it dawned on us: My husband and I both work at home, and the first thing our kids saw when they woke up and came to find us was Mom and Dad each typing away at a computer or talking on the phone. Instead of waking up to nurturing parents, Charlie was waking up to figures more focused on a screen than their sweet little boy. We figured out that if we stopped what we were doing and took five minutes to build a LEGO ship with him or give him undivided attention, then he'd be just fine. He needed our attention, to reconnect with us, and once he received it, he was happy to play independently. So we made a rule for the grown-ups: Get up earlier to get a head start on work if we need to, but the second we hear those little feet padding down the stairs, our computers and phones are put away and don't come back out until the kids have gone to school. Creating peaceful mornings for your children means starting out your own day in a thoughtful, mindful manner that can help carry you through the whole day. Getting up earlier allowed us to get a bit of our work out of the way, to allay our pressures, and then be truly engaged in building the most fabulous LEGO ship of all time when the chance arrived. And who doesn't want to take advantage of that opportunity?

Solutions: Peaceful Mornings

Early Childhood (ages 0–5)

- Keep your attention focused on your little one and provide a predictable routine. Put away computers and phones. If you need to, prepare lunches or shower the night before so you have more time in the morning for reading stories or even snuggling before everyone gets up.
- If you are at home with your child, try to plan an outing each day. A trip to a playground, library, or museum can be a wonderful way to spend the morning. On the way, play a "mindful seeing" game that challenges you and your child to notice something you both have never seen before. This simple activity is fun and helps engage us in present moment-to-moment awareness.
- Get the kids outside. Don't be afraid to bundle your little one up and get him outside. The fresh air is great for him and for you, and an outdoor environment is typically the perfect place

for kids to be creative. There they can make up new games and reap all the benefits of a healthy imagination.

- Try to build a morning walk into your routine.

Elementary (ages 5–10)

- Figure out what is calming or soothing for your kid, whether it's taking a morning bath or shower or eating a big breakfast, and build that activity into your morning routine. We want to send kids to school in a peaceful state of mind, so they are receptive to learning.
- If you can walk or bike to school, do it. Sometimes I'll drive to a spot and park and then walk the kids to school along a path, rather than deal with the crush of cars in the car pool lane.
- Be sure you allow adequate time for breakfast. Often breakfast gets forgotten when we run late. Sit down and eat with your kids.
- Get your kids in the habit of laying out clothes for the next day the night before to avoid morning wardrobe battles.
- Help your kids choose and pack their own lunches. This is also a good activity to do the evening before. Help your kids make their lunch right after dinner is finished, before the kitchen is cleaned up. It will make your morning go more smoothly and will be one less thing to clean up after the next day.

Tweens (ages 10–13)

- Encourage your child to get his things together and make his own lunch the night before so there's no last-minute search for homework or book bags or lacrosse sticks.

- Make a rule—and model it!—that the day starts with breakfast instead of with Facebook.
- If you drive them to school, let them pick a favorite song that you listen to together. This can help wake them up and put them in a good frame of mind on their way to school.
- Ask them a meaningful question about the day that awaits them, such as "What class might be the most challenging for you today?" and then see where the conversation heads.
- Try to avoid rehashing anything negative from the day or night before. If you have an unresolved argument, unless it is time-sensitive, let it go till after school, so your child is not sent off to school in a bad frame of mind.

Teens (ages 13–18)

- Most teens do not like getting up in the morning. Make certain everything they need for school is in place when they turn off their light at night.
- If you commute to school with your child, engage in meaningful conversation along the way. The car ride, if you can make it a phone-free zone, is a great opportunity for generating conversation.
- Make breakfast a time for connection. As kids get older and have more activities, it becomes harder to have regular family dinners. Wake up early and make them a yummy breakfast. Although they are old enough now to make their own breakfast, think of this as starting the day with an act of kindness. Sit with them, avoid the phones, and converse about the day to come.

FIVE

The Lost Art of Hanging Out

Y ou probably don't need me to tell you that kids are getting into organized sports at a younger and younger age. These days it's not uncommon to hear of three-year-olds playing soccer or basketball or hockey, and if your kid isn't playing T-ball as a toddler, then forget about the possibility of baseball later on. In chapter 4 we talked about the phenomenon of overscheduling, and organized sports is one of the worst culprits: Young kids can easily have three to four afternoons a week plus weekends filled with practices and games. In my talks, when I get to the discussion of organized sports, I always ask parents what their five-year-old's favorite part of playing organized sports is, what she talks about regarding her sport, and what she looks forward to the most. Unfailingly, they have the same response: the snack. It's not about dribbling or drills or even scoring a goal. No, it's all about the snack! Even if we are forcing our kids into unnatural social structures at young ages, it's comforting to me that their brains can still ferret out the part of organized activity that is totally age appropriate.

Some very important brain development occurs when kids are

young, but our increasing obsession with organized sports, and our decreasing free time in general, can be detrimental to that development. When I was growing up in Denver, every afternoon we'd play a pick-up game of soccer in the cul-de-sac with all the neighborhood kids. When kids play a pick-up game, a lot of important work takes place: They have to choose their teams fairly. They have to set boundaries for the game and decide on rules by which to play. For example, in my neighborhood the entire cul-de-sac was our field—nothing was out of bounds unless the ball rolled out into the busy street outside the cul-de-sac. Our garage door was one goal, and way at the other end of the cul-de-sac another garage door served as the opposing goal. At any time any player in the driveway in front of the goal could scoop up the ball and scream, "Goalie!" Those were our rules, and they worked for us. It involved planning, strategy, and cooperation. If a new kid wanted to join the game, we had to adapt. If there was a problem, we had to solve it. Each pick-up game involved planning, decision making, and problem solving—all functions of the prefrontal cortex, our thinking brains.

When kids play soccer on an organized team, by contrast, the rules are set, as are the boundaries, with the lines delineating the playing field literally drawn in place. The coach tells the kids what to do, and how to do it, and if there is a problem, the adults are quick to solve it.

The problem isn't that organized sports are bad, but that putting kids into organized sports at too early an age or for too much time during the week robs them of critical opportunities to learn how to solve problems on their own, make good choices, and deal with the consequences of poor choices or ones that don't work out as they thought they would. Free play, like those pick-up games, encourages creative expression. In fact, what kids do when they're not being told what to do is perhaps the core of childhood itself.

Opportunities for free play also happen when kids dress up and act out elaborate dramas or role-playing games, complete with sound effects or affected accents. They happen when kids play hopscotch on a playground or climb on the monkey bars; when they build block towers or LEGO spaceships; or when they become lost in drawing unicorn- and fairy-filled scenes. Free play is when a lot of critical brain development takes place.

What's Happening in the Brain

BUILDING WITH BLOCKS

To illustrate the rich cognitive development that free play encourages, let's look at the cognitive effects of a child playing with blocks or another construction-type toy. Though block play may seem like the simplest of activities, it is incredibly stimulating to the brain. While building castles and bridges and skyscrapers, a child develops spatial skills, motor skills, and hand-eye coordination. He engages in creative problem-solving to keep the structure from falling or to design the form he wants. If playing with other kids, he calls on social and language skills to communicate and engage. Kids who are encouraged to play with blocks or building toys, but who are not directed in their play, do even better in their ability to develop spatial skills. Some studies suggest that block play helps children develop skills that prime their brains for future language development, such as honing the ability to plan and recognize cause-and-effect scenarios: *If I put this block on top of that one, my bridge falls down. If I put a smaller block on top, it doesn't.*

Free play such as that involved in using building blocks also develops skills children use to play cooperatively with others, including that all-important skill empathy. When children play with others, there is an immediate need to coexist, and to be aware of how one's actions might affect those of the other child. If one child builds a tower that is too sprawling, it will interfere with her neighbor's ability to build freely or to have a positive experience. Way better than an electronic math "game," block playing is also associated with better math skills and builds problem-solving pathways in the brain. A 2011 longitudinal study tracked a group of kids from preschool all the way to high school. Even when controlled for IQ, the study found that kids who played with blocks in complex ways as preschoolers were more likely to do well in high school math and scored higher on standardized tests. All this from a bucket of blocks!

When a child plays with blocks, she also engages in what psychologists call divergent play. Divergent problems can be solved in lots of different ways, and thus are best solved by creative minds. Convergent problems, on the other hand, have only one correct answer or one solution, and thus don't require as much creative thinking. Studies show that divergent play (free play) prepares kids to think creatively and solve divergent problems, the more common type of problem we encounter in life. In one experiment, researchers gave kids either foam shapes or puzzle pieces and then gave them time to play. (Unlike foam shapes, puzzle pieces fit together in only one way, making puzzles a type of convergent play.) The kids were then tested on their ability to solve new types of problems. Those kids who played with the foam shapes were better able to creatively approach and solve the new tasks.

Free Play Is Under Attack

In 1997, the University of Michigan Institute for Social Research conducted a national study of 3,500 children age twelve and under and found that kids had half as much free time as they did thirty years prior. But instead of increasing opportunities for free play, every part of our success-oriented society, even sixteen years after the study, urges against it. Schools continue to pile on the homework load. Kids are directed into coach-led sports at earlier and earlier ages. While providing good opportunities for exercise and discipline, such sports do not allow kids to rely on their prefrontal cortexes—that's what being "coached" is all about, right? In addition, parents and families are being told that if you play a sport or want to become a violinist, in order to compete you have to do it 24/7, and to the exclusion of all other activities. Parents become convinced—and subsequently their kids become convinced—that kids cannot explore a sport or activity casually. Their commitment must not waiver, to the point where club sports now have camps for their teams that give the impression of being mandatory, and to participate in a dance recital, kids are strongly encouraged to attend a mini-camp before auditions are held. There are no sports seasons anymore; soccer players have to play twelve months out of the year if they're going to stay in the game. Free play and time just to hang around go right out the window.

Because of this attitude in our society—and because as parents we respond to this pressure by doing more, by scheduling our kids more—our children are losing the very *ability* to tap into the creative parts of their brains and express themselves. A preschool teacher in Steamboat Springs echoed these concerns to me, lamenting that even in preschool, "Kids don't know how to amuse themselves anymore." We've all seen this in action—kids who are "bored" or listless or whiny until they are either told exactly what to do and how to do it or are "plugged in" so they quite literally no longer have to think about what they might, or could, do with their time.

Even school recess, that bastion of free play, is under attack. A 2009 study conducted by researchers from the Albert Einstein College of Medicine's Department of Pediatrics found that only 30 percent of American students are granted adequate daily recess time. Some schools, especially those with low or falling test scores, have cut or reduced recess in order to give students more time in the classroom.

The recess study looked at eleven thousand elementary school children who were grouped based on the length of their daily recess. The study found that students who received more than fifteen minutes of free time each day showed markedly better behavior and greater focus than their peers who lacked recess. A little more than fifteen minutes of free time can improve concentration and focus, not to mention allowing children some much needed time and exercise outside. In 2009, Andrea Faber Taylor, a researcher from the University of Illinois, found that time outside in nature provides a true break from the classroom, preventing mental fatigue and making it easier to stay focused later in the day. Kids tend to engage in more vigorous activity when unleashed outdoors than they ever do in physical education classes.

Groups across the country, including the National Association of Early Childhood Specialists, have called for the return of recess as a way to improve concentration, reduce stress and anxiety in children, release energy, and help kids get physical. Recess and other free play forces children to learn to navigate social rules and constructs, teaches them independence, and encourages positive self-expression. This isn't news. Since the 1960s researchers have known that after rough-and-tumble play, and when allowed to explore their surroundings, test animals (rats) show increased brain levels of something called brain-derived neurotropic factor (BDNF). While it's a mouthful, BDNF is essential for the growth and main-tenance of brain cells, and higher levels are beneficial for the brain.

One study showed that Chinese and Japanese students, among the best academic achievers in the world, attend schools that pro-vide short breaks every hour. A British study of preschool-age children compared the capacity for children to engage in "sym-bolic" play by asking them to do tasks such as substitute a teddy bear for an absent object (an imaginative act much like making a doll into a fairy queen). The researchers found that those children who handled symbolic play more easily had better language skills. This was true both for "receptive" language, or what a child is able to understand or comprehend, and for "expressive" language, the words a child uses to express herself. It is clear that free play is incredibly important for young children, both cognitively and as a stress release.

The Lost Art of Hanging Out

In Denver, where I grew up, I moved to a new neighborhood in seventh grade and formed close friendships with a group of new friends. We spent the rest of junior high and high school in one another's company. We talked on the phone, we went to movies, but more than anything else we simply hung out.

I can't tell you what we did specifically, just that we "hung out," talking, joking, laughing, and even scheming. We met in parks, gazed at stars while lying on my friend's trampoline, retreated to basements, or just walked from one house to the next. We didn't have to annotate our communication with emoticons such as ;) or LOL to get across that we were just joking about something we'd just said. We could read one another's faces and know in a second if one of us had gone too far with a joke, or if one of us was having a really bad day. We talked a lot about nothing in particular, having conversations that might not have been important enough to post on Facebook but that helped forge bonds between us that have lasted to this day. The companions I found in the seventh grade are still my closest friends, the ones I never have to feel embarrassed in front of, the people I can share my most intimate stories with, the ones I wouldn't hesitate to call if I were in a real bind. I don't believe for a second that it was simply a quirk of fate and a bus stop that joined together such like-minded people. We forged our close bond by spending so much "ambient" time together. I'm talking about those experiences that are created when what is typically a five-minute walk home from school takes an hour, or when two or more people engage in unstructured chitter chatter while eating ice cream cones on park benches without the pressure of an upcoming activity hanging over us.

What my friends and I did—a whole lot of nothing in one another's company—is becoming increasingly rare. Just as younger kids are given LeapPads instead of being encouraged to play with blocks, older kids who meet at school these days keep tabs on one another online or through texts or e-mails. They may have incredible text-typing prowess, which my friends and I lacked, but they lack something far more important. As we learned in chapter 3, the neurological effects of "hanging out" virtually are distinct from those that result from goofing off with our friends in person. When we're online or scrutinizing our smartphones, our brains are busy trying to decode the lost nuance in electronic communication.

This happens to adults, too. We have all hesitated to reply to a text from a friend, not knowing whether she was joking or taking a deliberate jab. We've all puzzled over an e-mail from a co-worker, wondering whether the right response was to laugh conspiratorially or send a zinger right back as retribution. This sort of analysis is what every child is now doing neurologically, even when she doesn't realize it, when she "hangs out" with her friends and acquaintances in the world of social media. In short, writing on your friend's "wall" on Facebook (or whatever the next form of electronic communication is by the time you read this book!) is simply not the same as hanging out in a park or a basement or at the mall.

Unstructured time allows for critical brain development in younger kids. They learn to use the prefrontal cortex to solve problems, think creatively, adapt to changes, and make choices. For teens, problem solving becomes more about connection to others. When they are physically "hanging out" together, teens are learning to relate to one another, developing empathy through face-to-face interactions, and even figuring out what is attractive to them in a potential mate. In today's world, even when teens are in a room together, often they are still communicating with someone who isn't there. As a consequence, it is more difficult for them to develop mindfulness practices, because, for them, there is no present moment. (More on that later.) They also avoid negotiating uncomfortable social engagements they would otherwise have to confront face to face, and learn from. For example, teens can go to a party and, instead of having to muster the courage to go talk to someone, they can just hide and still look "cool" while standing in a corner with their cell phone. This shield thwarts personal social encounters, robbing teens of the critical skills they need as adults to navigate various social groups, whether it's part of their business or their social lives.

Is Overparenting Hurting Our Kids' Brains?

But if free play has all these cognitive benefits for our children, why don't we prioritize unstructured time for them? Nowadays, kids' activities are primarily structured and run by adults. Parents don't let their kids roam freely in the streets anymore, concerned as they are about predators and kidnappings. Some parents view this as a necessary response to the way society has changed, or argue that while they grew up in the suburbs, now they live in more crowded urban areas, with more crime and less space. Now if you let your kids run around without supervision, you could have Child Protective Services at your door.

But as *Free Range Kids* author and blogger Lenore Skenazy points out, that doesn't mean we're moving in the right direction. In her book and on her blog, Skenazy argues that not only is our nation's zealous overparenting rooted in dangerous fantasy instead of reality—kids are safer now than ever before; they are far more likely to be harmed by someone they know than kidnapped by a stranger—but we are crippling our children cognitively and socially when we don't allow them time to make mistakes and figure out solutions to their problems. Children don't learn how to be resourceful or how to solve their own problems unless they are given the opportunity to do so, including the opportunity to fail.

We have to find ways to let our kids play again—maybe with age-appropriate supervision, but not constant adult *direction*. We can move those neighborhood games from the front yards and streets into the backyards or to a park if we need to. We can take turns with other parents monitoring our kids as they play, without interfering too much. We can advocate for free time and recess as important parts of our kids' school days. We can work to give children as much choice as possible, even while educating them. For example, in the mindfulness classes I teach to students, I make mindfulness play-based. In the stories they "tell" through the mindful poses they choose, and through their creativity, a new story, *their* story, is born. There has been a small shift in "unscheduling" children due to an unlikely source. In 2010 a CBS News poll found that due to the recent economic recession, a third of parents have cut their kids' extracurricular activities because they were forced to do so for financial reasons. The silver lining is that while the motivation might have been financial difficulty, the results were nothing but positive. In a *Time* magazine poll, nearly four times as many people said their relationships with their children had gotten better since the recession hit.

As parents, we can help encourage creative, confident children in part by modeling for them the importance of free play, even for adults. If kids see and hear you call anything other than checking your e-mail or doing the laundry "wasting time," they won't believe that blowing dandelion fuzz or doing cartwheels is a worthy or appropriate endeavor. Take time to do art that speaks to you, whether it's knitting or woodworking or gardening. Prioritize riding bikes or taking walks. Take a moment to notice a glorious sunset or to watch the raindrops fall into a puddle, and point them out to your kid. Create a family game night, or even a poker night for older kids, and get serious about having fun. Parents can even schedule free time for our children just like we schedule date nights with our spouses, creating opportunities for connection and laughter. And make sure you listen to the messages you're sending your child about his "goofing off" or "being lazy." He might just be recharging his brain.

Solutions: Free Play and Hanging Out

Early Education (ages 0–5)

In an interview in *The Christian Science Monitor,* David Elkind, a child development professor and author of *The Hurried Child,* reminds parents that babies learn far more playing with a rattle than by watching *Baby Einstein.* Avoid giving young kids toys that don't require any imagination to make them interesting; battery-operated toys essentially play by themselves. In that spirit, help your little one by providing toys and opportunities that spark the imagination:

- Go to a big-box or thrift store the day after Halloween to buy dress-up clothes on the cheap, or contribute your own hats, belts, and scarves so kids can dress up.
- Look for toys endorsed by Waldorf or Montessori, instead of bowing to the commercial pressures of TV that have our kids screaming for the latest battery-operated toy that mimics a Disney movie. Waldorf and Montessori schools stress practical toys that are tactile, simple, and even contribute to later success by strengthening fine-motor skills.
- Puppets, train tracks and train tables, LEGOs and other building toys, and toy or extra dishes and cookware are all fun for kids this age.

Elementary (ages 5–10)

- Build time into your schedule and that of your school-age child for downtime. Just as you block out time to take her to soccer practice or him to piano lessons, schedule opportunities for your child to play in the park with friends, explore the ravine down the road, or read, write, or draw.

- Until the age of ten, limit organized sports to a maximum of two to three afternoons a week.

- Build an arts and crafts center in your house. Save those toilet paper rolls, egg cartons, and bubble wrap. Add tape or glue, a host of pens, some glitter or pompoms and get ready to be amazed.

- Let your child create magic "potions" out of ordinary kitchen ingredients, including vinegar, baking soda, lemon or almond extracts, spices, and fruit juices.

- Help your child plant a garden in the yard or in pots and keep him involved with the maintenance and the all-important harvesting. Vegetables such as snap peas, carrots, and corn are kid favorites, and make for ready-made outdoor snacks. You can even create living forts or secret spaces with tall sunflowers or peas or beans trained to climb tent-shaped poles.

- Older kids in this age range love playing board and card games, telling (bad!) jokes, doing puzzles, and learning (and performing) magic tricks.

- Let kids build a fort or play or sleep in a tent outside.

- Move up from holding "tea parties" to actually cooking and baking with your child.

- Get the pets in on the action. The cat might not appreciate getting dressed up, but the dog might like being brushed and groomed, taking a walk, playing fetch, or going swimming.

- Encourage your kids to write and direct their own plays or shows. Kids can fill an entire afternoon with this one, and they will love the chance to perform for you.

How to Play Those Games You Forgot About

One of the best things you can do for your kids is teach them and their friends how to play classic kid games. Even teens can get excited by Capture the Flag (especially if they play against adults), while Duck, Duck, Goose is a fave with the preschool set. If you don't quite remember exactly how these games are played, here are the rules of some favorites:

CAPTURE THE FLAG

Divide the playing field in two "camps." Each team gets its own flag (or other object), which is in plain view toward the back of each camp. Players on each team must try to break into "enemy territory" and bring the opposing team's flag back to their own home base. In their half of the field, players cannot be tagged, but once they enter the other team's camp, they're at risk— anyone on the other team can tag them and send them to "jail" (a predetermined spot not very close to the flag).

There are variations, but one way to get out of jail is to have someone on your own team perform a "jailbreak"—get into the jail and tag you to release you.

DUCK, DUCK, GOOSE

This classic game starts when one person goes around a circle of kids gently touching everyone's head and saying, "Duck . . . duck . . . duck . . ." Eventually, the child chooses one person to be the "goose." When she calls out, "Goose!" the chosen child has to get up and chase the leader around the circle. If the "goose" catches her, then the leader has to start again, and the goose sits down. If the goose misses, the leader hurries to the empty spot in the circle, and the goose is the new leader. continues until everyone gets a turn.

GHOST IN THE GRAVEYARD (OR SARDINES)

Start with the idea of hide-and-seek, then turn it around. Instead of there being one person who counts and a bunch of people who hide, Ghost in the Graveyard features one person who hides (the ghost) while everyone else counts. Everyone stands together with eyes closed and backs turned, slowly counting the hours—"One o'clock, two o'clock, three o'clock"—until they get to midnight. Then they yell, "Midnight! I hope the ghost isn't out tonight!" (or something to that effect).

Everyone then goes off in search of the ghost, who can decide to pop out of hiding at any moment and tag "victims." When someone spots the ghost, he yells, "Ghost in the graveyard!" and everyone flees as fast as they can back to base. If the ghost tags anyone, that person (or people) is the ghost in the next round. Otherwise, the same person plays the ghost again, or kids can choose a new ghost.

If the name or idea of ghosts is too scary for young kids, there are many variations, including Sardines. Sardines begins the same way, with a group of kids counting and then searching for one hidden child, or "sardine." The difference is that when someone finds this child, instead of yelling and running, she hides with the child. This continues until everyone has found the hiding space and is packed together in it (like sardines, naturally).

HIDE-AND-SEEK

Okay, you probably remember this one, but try playing it at a park instead of in your house. And do you remember that a shout of "Olly olly oxen free" means that everyone can come out of hiding?

cont.

RED LIGHT, GREEN LIGHT

Much more fun than actually being in traffic, this game involves one child standing at one end of a room or expanse of ground and the other children—it can be any number of children, from two up—standing about twenty-five feet away. The first child calls out, "Green light!" and turns her back for a short time. During a "green light," the kids are allowed to run or walk quickly toward her. When she turns back toward them and says, "Red light!" the kids are supposed to anticipate this and freeze in place before she turns fully around. If she catches anyone moving, that person is "out." The game continues until someone successfully tags the leader and takes her place.

RED ROVER

You need a large group for this one, but it's fun and builds team spirit. The kids split themselves up into two equal-size teams. Each team lines up side to side, holding hands, with arms outstretched at about forty-five—degree angles. The two teams need to be facing each other, with a large stretch of space in between them. One team calls out, "Red Rover, Red Rover, let [child's name] come over."

The invited child runs toward the other team with as much force as she can, trying to break through the link between any two players on the opposing team. If she does, she gets to go back to her own team along with an opposing team member of her choice, who then joins her team. If she doesn't break through, she is "caught" and stays on the opposing team. The game is over when all the children are on the same team.

TELEPHONE

Some of you might remember this game as being called Operator, but it might take longer to explain to your child what an operator once was than to explain the rules! In this game, everyone sits in a circle. One person, the leader, thinks of a phrase or sentence to whisper to the person to the right of him. That person must then whisper the phrase to the person to the right of him, and so on, until it reaches the leader again. There are usually no "repeats" allowed—the idea is that players have to do the best they can to figure out what the person whispered, and the phrase can get very convoluted as it goes down the line. When the last person has heard the whisper, she says it out loud, and then gets to come up with the next phrase or sentence to whisper around the group.

   To find more ideas for group games for kids (or more details about the ones I've just described), try any of these websites:

* spoonful.com/family-fun
* www.gameskidsplay.net
* www.best-kids-games-online.com
* www.group-games.com

Tweens (ages 10–13)

David Elkind offers a word of advice to parents of tweens: Don't get your feelings hurt if your child would prefer "playing" with his friends rather than with you. You can stay on the periphery and keep an eye on things by helping create a home where your child and his friends like to hang out, but don't intrude.

- Take your kids and their friends mountain biking, skiing, hiking, to the beach, or camping; take them to a skate park or park.
- Reward creativity with more autonomy and control. Let your tween and a friend go farther from the house to play at a park or ride their bikes. Let them create and cook their own dinner menu or breakfast on the weekends. Let them program your dinner music or create a playlist for the tunes you play in the car.
- Instead of letting them stay glued to YouTube, have them create, direct, and record their own video. This is a great way to balance their love of technology with creativity and dramatic play.

Teens (ages 13–18)

It can be difficult to help teens carve out time for fun in their increasingly busy schedules. In fact, it might be parents' first impulse to tell their teen to quit goofing off and get going on the homework! But remember those studies that show that without any downtime your teen won't be more successful; in fact, she might be less so. Embrace being the fun one sometimes instead of the homework and chore taskmaster and set a good example for your teen by not embracing the all-work-and-no-play lifestyle yourself.

- Even if you lack a basement (or trampoline) and are crammed into a tiny apartment, you can help your teen by creating a home where other kids feel welcome coming over and hanging out. Plan and cook big dinners with your teens and have them invite their friends over to eat. Create movie nights where the teens get to pick the movie and you make the popcorn.

- Support your teen's passion, whether it's jewelry making or creative writing or noodling on the bass guitar.
- Try to create a space in the home where teens can have independence but still have fun stuff to do. Maybe the kids can play cards or trivia games or board games. They might have access to a pool table (or an actual pool, if you're lucky enough to live someplace warm) or a foosball or Ping-Pong table. Set up an interactive game system, or let your kids soundproof your garage so they can jam.
- Encourage kids to explore the world of pick-up sports. Help them plan out mountain biking routes, have them go to the skate park, or send them to play basketball at a community center. Take your teen and a friend with you to the slopes or on a hike.
- Have older kids hang out with younger ones. Little kids who know how to play unabashedly are great at getting older kids to shrug off their self-consciousness and remind them how much fun play can be.

SIX

The Simple Power of **Sleep**

Disrupted sleep is a clear indicator that your life is out of balance. When we're worried, we can't sleep at night, or we wake up in a panic. When we're depressed, we sleep too much. Before they learn how to regulate their sleep, infants keep us up with crying and midnight feedings. Then restless teenagers keep us up while we wait for them to come home safely from an evening out! But there is a much more common and less recognized problem with sleep in so many of our kids' lives. Sleep is the root cause of some common critical behavioral problems, and too little sleep can have serious deleterious effects on growing and developing brains.

Last summer I was at the end of my rope with my son Charlie. Summer is supposed to be a lazy, easy-going time—peaceful, slow. In summertime the stars should align to reduce automatically the stress of an average family—or so goes the conventional wisdom. Well, instead, I was dealing with a five-year-old who couldn't stay focused on any one task long enough to get his shoes tied or his teeth brushed. He'd started having crazy temper tantrums, and was downright defiant most of the time. He was argumentative with me and his father, was super touchy, and his temper was quick to escalate. He was irritable, totally unlike himself, and such a bear—especially in the mornings—that I grew to dread waking up and starting our days. I was so confused by his complete change in personality that my psychologist brain kicked in and I started running through the usual suspects: ADHD, Sensory Integration Disorder, even Oppositional Defiance Disorder (ODD) ran through my mind. At least they offered some explanations for what Charlie was going through.

Somehow we made it through the summer, and with fall the kids went back to school. We all settled in to our usual routines, including set bedtimes that were about an hour and a half earlier than those during the summer. Well, guess what happened. As if by magic, my lovely boy returned. He was pleasant and focused (as much as a five-year-old ever is), and happily did what he was asked (most of the time). It was only then that it hit me what had happened to Charlie. That summer we had had fun. We rode our bikes to late concerts in the park, dragging ourselves home after ten o'clock. We hung out on the porch, enjoying the warmer temperatures and the lingering evening light while the kids played outside. In short, we went to bed late and still got up early, not an uncommon summertime phenomenon. When imposed routines such as school go out the window, too often so do routines such as fixed bedtimes. But what felt like fun was taking its toll on Charlie, as we whittled away more and more precious hours of rest. You know how you feel as an adult when you stayed out too late the night before and have to drag yourself into the office, red-eyed, coffee clutched in your hands. Well, the effects on kids are even more dire. On average, children today get an hour less sleep than kids did thirty years ago, and we are paying a price. Dropping below eight hours of sleep doubles your kid's chance of becoming clinically depressed. Even his school work will suffer. In a 2001 study of high school students that looked at the correlation between sleep habits and grades, researchers found that teens who received As averaged about fifteen minutes more sleep than B students, who in turn received fifteen minutes more sleep than C students—are you detecting a pattern yet? While we sleep, our brains are actually very busy doing important work that affects our waking hours to a significant degree (beyond making us feel funny until that first cup of coffee). Here's a closer look at what's going on behind those closed eyelids.

What's Happening in the Brain

Sleep is so critical to humans that it's the primary activity of our brains during infancy. The sleep-wake cycle is part of what are called our circadian rhythms, or those physical, mental, and behavioral changes that follow a roughly twenty-four-hour cycle. The rhythms are generally guided by our exposure to light and dark, which is why we sleep at night and are active during the day. It takes humans a while to develop regular patterns that respond to light and dark, which is why newborns have such wonky sleep schedules. At some point in the range of three to six months of age, newborns' bodies regulate these cycles and develop a more predictable and stable sleep pattern.

Our brains' "master clock," the suprachiasmatic nucleus, or SCN, is a nerve control center that coordinates our circadian rhythms. The SCN is located in the hypothalamus, a part of the limbic system that's located near our old friend the amygdala, in an area of the brain near the optic nerves. Light, registered by our optic nerves, is the main environmental indicator that cues changes in our circadian rhythms. When there is less light, the SCN prompts the brain to produce more of a hormone called melatonin, which makes us sleepy (and, of late, has been synthesized and sold as a sleep aid). More light, and the SCN tells the brain to ease up on the production of melatonin. Those changes in turn affect our sleep-wake cycles, impact the release of certain hormones, and alter our body temperature.

Our time spent sleeping is put to very good use by our brain, which takes full advantage of the body's downtime to catch up. Information taken in during the day is processed and organized while we sleep; you could say this is when the information actually "sinks in." This is also why it's counterintuitive to keep a younger child up doing homework instead of sending her to bed to get the right amount of shut-eye. In one study, fourth-graders went home with randomly drawn instructions either to go to bed earlier or to stay up later, for three nights. Each child wore a monitor to gauge activity, enabling researchers to see how much sleep the child was actually getting. After the third night's sleep, a researcher went to the school to give each child a test of neurobiological functioning. The researchers found that the performance gap caused by an hour's difference in sleep was bigger than the gap between a normal fourth-grader and a normal sixth-grader. Or, to restate it in plain terms, a slightly sleepy sixth-grader will perform in class like a fourth-grader.

Sleep is particularly important for kids. During sleep, the brain shifts what it learned that day to more efficient storage regions. During this process, neural connections along learning pathways are strengthened, positive memories are enhanced, and inferences and associations are drawn. Interrupted sleep disrupts this entire process. The more you are learning (as an active fourth-grader is), the more you need to sleep.

Did you know that children two years old and under have spent more time sleeping than they have awake? Overall, most children spend a full 40 percent of their childhoods snoozing away, which gives them a critical opportunity to shape their mental and physical development.

This processing time is also the reason you may wake up to what my husband and I call the Hour of Doom—when you lie awake, often at four o'clock in the morning, in sheer panic, cycling through everything on your to-do list that you haven't done and those things you didn't do as well as you wanted to, or worrying about what you won't do. or won't do as well as you want to, in your entire life. Before you reach for the anxiety meds, you should understand that your disrupted sleep (or lack of sleep) is probably behind this stream of negativity. Negative stimuli get processed by the amygdala, while positive memories get processed by the hippocampus. Sleep deprivation affects the hippocampus much more than it does the amygdala, with the result that sleep-deprived people are flush with negative memories and associations, and have more difficulty recalling memories that are good or pleasant.

Though you might not be able to tell from looking at a sleeping child, all humans engage in two different types of sleep phases. The first is non-rapid eye movement (NREM), or "quiet" sleep. This is the deep sleep during which our muscles receive increased blood supply and our "batteries" are "recharged" due to increased energy flow and tissue growth and repair. Deep sleep is also when our bodies release hormones that are important for growth and development.

More people are aware of what is called rapid eye movement (REM) sleep. This is active sleep, during which our brains are alert and active, and it is the time when we dream. Our heart rates and breathing patterns become irregular during this phase of sleep. By the time kids are six months old, they spend about 30 percent of their total sleep time in REM sleep.

So, What's a Little Sleep?

To kids, getting enough sleep is incredibly important, and there are far greater repercussions to their not doing so than having to deal with a grumpy pain-in-the-you-know-what kid. Kids who don't get enough sleep are more likely to be obese, have problems with attention, underperform in school, and suffer from anxiety and depression. Though we are often hypervigilant about how much infants sleep and can recite our toddler's complicated nap schedule, as kids get older, most parents (including me, as is evident by my story about Charlie) get more lax.

The National Sleep Foundation recommends that kids ages five to twelve get ten to eleven hours of sleep a night. This means that if your child needs to wake up at 7:00 A.M. to get ready for the school day, he should be *asleep* by 9:00 P.M. at the minimum; 8:00 P.M. would be even better. This usually means starting the bedtime routine an hour before bedtime, if there is to be time to relax; to perform any comforting routines such as reading or listening to music; or to complete necessary activities such as brushing teeth.

We have learned that kids today sleep an average of an hour less a night than kids did thirty years ago, and as we examined in the previous chapters, it's no wonder when we look at our over-stimulated, overscheduled lives. Our kids experience increasing demands on their free time, and between homework, organized sports, and the pull of TV and the Internet, it's a wonder some of them sleep at all! Add in energy drinks and caffeinated soda, and the stimulation of screen time, and we start to see more difficulty falling asleep, increased nightmares, and other sleep disruptions. In particular, studies show that watching TV close to bedtime makes kids more unwilling to go to bed, causes them difficulty falling asleep, increases the anxiety some kids have around sleep, and results in fewer hours spent sleeping on the whole.

Television is part of the reason sleep disorders are so prevalent for school-age kids. Such disorders lead to mood swings, hyper-activity, or cognitive problems that impact their ability to learn. Research shows a major impact from even small amounts of lost sleep, including resulting underperformance in school, depres-sion, and anxiety. Not getting enough sleep also increases the risk of obesity. It is counterintuitive to think that a sedentary activity such as getting more sleep would actually decrease a child's risk of obesity, but that is the result. Too little or interrupted sleep disrupts the production of the hormones that regulate hunger and fat production. Your body increases production of ghrelin, the hormone that tells you you're hungry, and decreases production of leptin, our natural appetite suppressant. Net result: increased eating. Too little sleep also elevates cortisol, a stress hormone that acts in part to signal your body to make fat. In 2010, a study pub-lished in the *Archives of Pediatrics and Adolescent Medicine* linked a lack of adequate sleep in infants and young children with an in-creased likelihood of obesity later in life. Dr. Janice F. Bell of the

University of Washington found that kids under five and babies who didn't sleep enough at night—naps didn't seem to affect the outcome—were more likely to become overweight or obese. The researchers hypothesized that the brain was affected by the lack of sleep, which disrupted the regulation of tiredness and the metabolism. In 2011, an article published in a pediatric journal found that data from twenty-nine studies across sixteen countries associate inadequate sleep and late bedtimes with an increased risk for being or becoming overweight or having increased body fat.

Though well documented, obesity isn't the only issue; the link between inadequate sleep and depression in kids is clear. Students who get more sleep report higher levels of motivation and lower levels of depression, while dropping below eight hours of sleep *doubles* the rate of clinical depression. According to research studies published in the journal *Sleep* and examined by the National Sleep Foundation, kids and adolescents with depression suffer from sleep problems such as an inability to sleep, insomnia, or excessive sleepiness (what is called hypersomnia). In addition, children who have sleep problems also have more severe depression or depression that is longer lasting. A National Sleep Foundation poll focusing on tween and teens found nearly three-quarters (73 percent) of those adolescents who reported being unhappy were also not sleeping adequate amounts at night. Persistent sleep problems in children, such as not getting enough sleep or having sleep cycles interrupted, can be even more severe, and have been associated with a depressed mood or an inability to feel pleasure, one of the hallmark symptoms of depression.

The Myth of the Lazy Teenager

It's a common scenario for any parent of a teen: It has just struck noon on a Saturday and you're staring at a closed bedroom door. Your teenager isn't yet awake, though the rest of you have been at it for hours. You're sure that if you don't wake her, she'll happily sleep the day away. What happens to teenagers to make them this lazy? You know they can get up early—they do it five days a week to get to school, then stay busy all day with football practice and soccer. And they love to stay up into the wee hours. So why can't they be present on the weekends? Has your teen turned into a zombie? Is she just trying to avoid having to talk to you?

The answer may be twofold. First, your teen isn't getting enough sleep during the week. Second, on the weekends, absent a fixed early wake time, he is simply following his own internal clock. We long believed that teenagers, no longer being young kids, needed the same amount of sleep as their parents. And while it's true that adolescents sleep less than younger kids, they need more sleep, and they sleep on a different rhythm, than you do. While a quarter of high school students regularly sleep less than 6.5 hours on school nights, studies show that adolescents need about 9.2 hours of sleep each night, compared with the 7.5 to 8.0 hours parents should be getting to feel rested.

In addition puberty causes a shift in the natural rhythms of teens and tweens. Teens aren't just staying up to text their friends when you're not around; they are biologically driven to become drowsy later in the evening than adults or than younger kids. Studies have linked the physical maturation of kids to shifts in melatonin production, the hormone that helps make us sleepy. These studies suggest that the brain's circadian rhythms are al-

What a Difference an Hour Makes

One of the most difficult hurdles for teens in getting enough sleep is dealing with school. Yes, they have hours of homework at night, but due to reduced bus resources and in order to best use facilities and shared staff, the start times for high school have been creeping earlier and earlier, with 7:15 not uncommon. Add in the time kids need to get ready and to travel to school, and there is simply no way that kids with normal extracurricular activities can get enough rest. Some school districts are trying to change that.

Following the release of a Minnesota Medical Association resolution titled Sleep Deprivation in Adolescents, the school districts in Edina and Minneapolis have changed the start times in their schools. In Minneapolis, for example, school schedules were shifted from 7:15 A.M.–1:45 P.M. to 8:40 A.M.–3:20 P.M.

The Center for Applied Research and Educational Improvement (CAREI) at the University of Minnesota studied the impact of these changes on academic performance, behavior, and safety in urban and suburban schools. In both Edina and Minneapolis the schedule shifts resulted in improved attendance, an increase in continuous enrollment (decreased dropouts), less tardiness, and fewer trips to the school nurse. Not only that, but kids had "gained" about an hour, enough to report being able to eat breakfast in the morning and have time during the school day—not at 2:00 A.M.—to finish homework, which they could do because they were more alert.

CAREI's study found it difficult to assess changes in grades due to too many variables in grading policy and other factors, but the suburban teachers and principals reported that students seemed more alert and calmer, and there were fewer trips to the principal's office. Both urban and suburban parents

cont.

said their kids were easier to get along with, more conversational, and less combative. Similar experiments in Massachusetts found clear academic benefits for a school with later start times when compared to a similar school that started an hour earlier, and later start times in Kentucky even reduced the collision rate for young drivers: the crash rate in one county for sixteen- to eighteen-year-olds dropped following the change in start times, while crash rates for seventeen- to eighteen-year-olds actually rose in the rest of the state during the same time period.

tered in conjunction with physical changes in the teen's body, with the melatonin "switch" being thrown later at night as puberty and development progress. This later sleep time is why teens have difficulty waking early and being alert. Most teens, however, are facing earlier start times than ever for school and sports, with no correlating change in bedtime. The results are insufficient sleep, difficulties in learning, disciplinary problems, sleepiness in class, and an inability to concentrate and focus. The effects on kids' academic performance is also striking. *Just an hour a day makes all the difference:* A Brown University Medical School study found that students earning Cs, Ds, and Fs on their report cards got about twenty-five minutes less sleep and went to bed about forty minutes later than their peers getting As and Bs.

Of course, lower grades aren't the most important factor for sleep-deprived kids; their very brains are being put at risk, as is their ability to regulate emotion and behavior. In addition to depression, studies show links between sleep deprivation and ADHD, and more generalized difficulty controlling emotion and impulses, which can potentially lead to risky behavior.

How to Help Your Kids Get More Sleep

Don't worry! One of the best aspects of sleep being such a critical component to developing a healthy brain is that it's also a
relatively easy issue to remedy. You may discover, as I did, that
all sorts of behavior issues or acting out on the part of your child
are due to lack of sleep and routine, and that once your child is
on a good regimen you will all see the benefits. While lack of
sleep produces ill effects, good sleep patterns elicit positive ones.
While you may not be able to change the start time of your kid's
high school, beginning when your child is young to inculcate
good sleep habits is a great step forward. In my talks and classes
(as well as at home), I use what I call the R.E.S.T. program to
help establish good habits and make bedtime an easier transition
for everyone.

Let's Get Some R.E.S.T.

R.E.S.T. is one of the most powerful frameworks I have in my
toolbox in talking with parents about how to regulate their kids'
bedtime schedules. R.E.S.T. stands for Routine, Empowerment,
Snuggle Time, and Teaching Children to Relax. Taken together,
R.E.S.T. is extremely effective for kids and can transform bedtime into a lovely transition from a busy day. Though R.E.S.T. is
geared toward younger children, as we go through it, you will
see that some of the elements work just as well for tweens and
even teenagers. Your fifteen-year-old might not be angling to
snuggle, but you can still build in time to connect with him before bed. I have a friend who stays up until 11:30 (even though

she is ready to go to bed at 9:00) because she knows that her teens are open to talking and connecting before they sleep. We'll speak more toward the end of the chapter about solutions for different ages, but first, it's all about the routine.

ROUTINE

You will feel instant effects if you take the time when your kids are young to create a healthy bedtime routine and use it consistently. The ritual of a healthy routine prepares children's minds and bodies for sleep. When children know what to expect they are much less likely to resist changes and can easily transition from one activity to the next. Unpredictability, on the other hand, can cause feelings of anxiety, and the result is resistance. A healthy routine starts with dinner and can include playtime, bathtime, clean-up of toys, an evening snack, reading or looking at books, snuggle time, and other soothing activities. Especially for younger kids but also for older ones, limit screen time, especially after dinner! Even "educational" programs can elicit a stress response in your child's brain, making it more difficult for her to fall asleep easily. Once a healthy routine is established it is easier to enter the routine partway through when you need to. For example, if you have dinner at a friend's house and return home late one night, you might have to jump right into snuggle time or reading. You will find that this works better when your children follow a routine most of the time and are familiar with the pattern.

EMPOWERMENT

When children begin to realize they are independent beings, they develop a need for control. They want to establish their independence and they do this by trying to control as many situations as they can. While this can be challenging for parents (incredibly challenging at times!), it is a normal part of development. By offering your child the opportunity to take on a leadership role in a developmentally appropriate way, you can satisfy his desires, build his self-esteem, and, most important, avoid a whole lot of power struggles. There are many opportunities to empower your children during their nightly bedtime routine.

◆ Let your child help create the routine (with a little guidance of course). For children who are unable to read, lay out pictures of the elements you would like to include in the routine (dinner, playtime, bath, brushing teeth, reading, etc.), and let them create their own chart for nightly events. Ideally, children can complete homework prior to dinner, but if not, include this in the routine. Allowing your child to help create the routine gives her the control she wants and increases her desire to follow a schedule. When it is time to transition from one activity to the next, ask her, "What is next?" My daughter loves to explain the chart, very knowledgeably, to babysitters!

◆ Give young children lots of opportunities to make choices. Offer them two options, both of which will be okay even if they do the choosing. For example, "Would you like to pick up the LEGOs first or the train tracks?" or "Would you like to wear the red pajamas or the blue ones?" or "Would you like to have an apple or a banana for your snack?" One of my favorites: "Would you like to go to bed now or in ten minutes?" The secret is to plan ahead and ask this question about fifteen minutes prior to the child's actual bedtime. You know what the answer will be, but again, giving him some control can go a long way toward preventing power struggles.

SNUGGLE TIME

As we saw in the first chapter, our experience as children was vastly different from that which children face today. With each generation, the amount of face-to-face engagement children have with adults decreases. As families spread out across the country, we see less of the multigenerational homes that once were commonplace. Neighborhoods become less communal, and children don't run freely from one home to the next as they once did. Student-to-teacher ratios continue to increase, and most children prefer to interact with their peers through text messages or e-mails rather than have in-person conversations. Yet research in the field of resiliency points to the child's relationship with a caring adult figure as the *most critical protective factor* a child can have against the challenges he will inevitably face, big challenges such as deciding whether to try drugs, have sex, or get in a car with a driver who has been drinking. Research shows that children who feel more connected to the adults in their lives make better choices. If it's difficult to get face-to-face time other times during the day, take the opportunity offered by your "captive" bedtime audience to spend some really quality one-on-one time with your kid.

This time can be spent reading books and discussing them, singing songs, telling stories, or simply snuggling and cuddling. Taking time each night to connect with your child in this way will play a critical role in the choices she makes, the goals she achieves, and her relationships in general as she grows. Additionally, this close bonding helps children develop empathy, a natural means of handling the stress response in their own bodies.

TEACHING CHILDREN TO RELAX

Relaxation is the key element I find missing in many suggested bedtime routines. A great routine can make bedtime go smoother, but often it is not enough to help your little one fall asleep. In a go, go, go world it is difficult for us to turn off our minds so we can relax and fall asleep. Just as you spend time tossing and turning worrying about the meeting you have the next day, the constant stimulation of living in a modern world has most children's brains in a constant state of fight, flight, or freeze. Learning relaxation skills early will provide your young child with lifelong benefits.. Research has shown that learning effective relaxation skills can not only calm the stress response and help him sleep, but also increase stimulation in areas of the brain related to attention, memory, and learning. See the solutions sections for tips on how to teach your kids relaxation techniques. Read through the later chapters on mindfulness for more tools for building relaxation into your child's life in a more systematic way.

Solutions: Sleep

Early Learning (ages 0–5)

- Enough has been written on how to get your baby to sleep to fill the Grand Canyon, so I will not detail any tips or tools for getting your infant to sleep. Two helpful titles that I especially like include *On Becoming BabyWise* and *Healthy Sleep Habits, Happy Child*. In general, suggestions that work for older kids also work for babies, including developing regular schedules, creating conducive sleep spaces, and teaching children to soothe themselves or relax.

- Even once your baby can walk, recognize that toddlers still need a lot of sleep, somewhere between twelve and fourteen hours a day, including naps and nighttime sleeping.

- Try not to put toddlers down for naps too close to bedtime, as it might cause problems putting them to bed at the usual time.

- Stick to a routine for your toddler (R.E.S.T.). This helps make bedtime smoother for the whole family and teaches your little one good sleep habits. There's nothing quite as nice as snuggling with a toddler, either!

- Preschoolers typically sleep eleven to thirteen hours each night. Because most kids stop napping once they reach kindergarten, this means you need to ensure they are receiving the right amount of sleep at night.

- Kids this age can have trouble falling asleep or they wake up during the night. Establishing a good routine and teaching your kids a mindfulness practice will help them get themselves to (and back to) sleep without your intervention. Because nightmares are common, limit scary talk and especially scary programs or books right before bed, and be mindful of what they are exposed to during the day. Their imaginations run wild, and they soak in everything they hear.

- The Mindful Life Dreamzzz CDs (available at http://www .mindfullifetoday.com/category_s/49.htm) teach children these skills in a developmentally appropriate way, allowing children to learn how to relax their muscles and their minds so they can fall asleep easily. They also learn valuable relaxation skills that they can use anytime they need them.

Elementary (ages 5–10)

- Continue to use the R.E.S.T. patterns established when your kids were younger. (Relish cuddling the older ones—that won't last for long!)
- Keep bedrooms cool, dark, and technology-free
- Don't let kids watch TV or use the computer right before going to bed. Keep cell phones, computers, and televisions out of the bedroom.

Tweens and Teens (ages 10–18)

- Talk to tweens and teens about the effects of having too little sleep and educate them on how much sleep they need.
- Try to add just fifteen minutes of sleep. Explain to your tween/teen the study regarding the correlation between the amount of sleep one gets and the grades he receives—kids who get fifteen minutes more sleep achieve higher grades—and then brainstorm solutions for getting those extra minutes. Ideas may include prepping more the night before and getting some extra Zs in the morning, or starting a bedtime routine earlier.
- In some schools, teens have flexibility in the scheduling of their classes. If possible, have them schedule the first class of the day as an off period, so they can get more sleep. (Be sure to keep their bedtime the same!) But keep in mind that this will require them to arrange alternative transportation to school.
- Give your tweens and teens mindfulness exercises and teach them how to calm their own bodies through meditation, visualization, and even yoga.

- Continue to emphasize the need for a regular and consistent sleep schedule and bedtime routine. Allow your tween or teen to sleep in on the weekends if he needs it.
- Keep bedrooms cool, dark, and quiet. Invest in blackout shades for the summer to help him sleep in the mornings.
- Keep TVs, computers, and cell phones out of the bedroom. Charge them overnight in a central location, in the family room, or near your room, to help your teen avoid temptation.
- With the advent of "energy drinks," kids are drinking loads of sugar and caffeine in new and concentrated ways. Limit (or eliminate) the caffeine.

PART III

Mindfulness: Increasing Your Inner Resiliency

SEVEN

Finding Your Own Meditation

Recently, I arrived home after traveling for ten days in a row. I had been away training instructors to teach mindfulness to kids, providing workshops for parents on "Creating Peaceful Homes," and helping teachers create classroom environments in which kids were calm, prepared, and ready to learn. I was, as my presentations talk about, "sowing the seeds of peace and happiness" everywhere I went. That said, though the trip was successful, it felt like a very, very long time to be away from my family. I couldn't wait to get home and see my husband and kids.

Well, it took about an hour and fifteen minutes after my return home for me to forget everything I'd been preaching to others over the previous ten days. Instead of basking in a blissful reunion with my happy family, I found myself confronting conflict: While we were sitting around the dinner table, one of the kids threw the new toy I had just brought home across the table at the other. The two screamed, fought, and whined. And what were my husband and I doing? We found ourselves screaming, fighting, and whining right along with them. I eventually sent both kids to their rooms, wondering why I had been so excited to get home in the first place.

Yep, it happens in our household, too. No matter how much we might know about kids, psychology, or parenting, we have those moments where it all goes out the window. Shortly after my happy homecoming, I met with a colleague to discuss an upcoming expert panel we were to appear on together. She told me that when people ask her, "What's the secret to parenting?"—a very common question for any parenting "expert"—she simply says, "Be the person you want your kids to become."

It's simple, but it's so true. If you want to raise compassionate, caring, kind kids, then you must model compassion, caring, and kindness toward others. If you want your kids to have high self-esteem, then model self-care and speak kindly about yourself. If you want your kids to overcome adversity, push yourself out of your comfort zone and let them observe you facing your fears and striving toward new goals. Finally, if you want your kids to know it is okay to make mistakes, you need to acknowledge once in a while that you make them, too.

Connecting back to my story, I want to assure you that we all make mistakes. When we do, however, it is so easy as a parent to blame these breakdowns on our kids' behavior, or on our spouse, our work, or a host of other outside influences. I know, because it happens to me, too. I try to remember how important it is to acknowledge when you've made a mistake or acted poorly. If we can't acknowledge our mistakes in front of our kids, or apologize to them when we haven't done the right thing, then we are missing an opportunity to send a powerful message. If we want our kids to hold themselves accountable for their mistakes and to make it right when they have done something wrong, then we need to model this behavior ourselves. In chapter 4, I told you that you can't pluck the phone out of your texting tween's hand while holding your own smartphone, answering an e-mail while you do it. It's not only hypocritical but also ineffective. In chapter 5, I said that while the effects of sleep deprivation on your child are especially critical, if you aren't getting enough sleep or good sleep, either, then no one in your family is functioning well. In short, modeling good behavior around the use of technology, scheduling, prioritizing creativity and self-care goes a long way toward helping your children change their behavior in these areas. But in order to model this behavior, we have to be in the right place to act intentionally, with our best selves.

There are two main ways to create the sense of peace we need to be our best selves—that is, to be those parents who take responsibility and own up to it when we haven't done our best, and who do our best more often. The first way is to control or remove those external things that cause us stress. In part 2 we focused on addressing and removing some of the most common external stressors in our lives. As families, we need to pay attention to and regulate our sleep. We need to take care not to overschedule ourselves or our children, and make sure we're scheduling in downtime or time for free play. We need to be intentional in our use of technology and spend more time with one another than we spend in front of screens of any type. Making changes to these external factors goes a long way toward helping us find balance.

But no matter what we do, we'll face stress—unexpected challenges, particularly busy times. We can't control for every variable, no matter how much we try. So we must work to foster a peaceful frame of mind. We need strategies for building up our internal resiliency so that when stress does come along, as it inevitably will, we have the tools to manage it effectively. In the chapters that follow I'll talk about how to create a mindful family whose members can develop tools to be present and in tune with their own emotions and responses. I'll talk about how to cultivate abundant gratitude and ensure that family members aren't stuck on a wheel of negativity. I'll provide tips for raising hardworking, motivated children and for increasing empathy. I'll give you and your children skills for how to employ and enjoy a mindfulness practice in your everyday lives. And we'll talk about channeling children's need for excitement into spine-tingling adventures rather than risky behaviors. It's all great stuff, but the first step to building that resiliency requires putting your full attention toward your own self-care in three key areas: giving attention to and improving your relationship with your partner, caring for your brain and body through physical exercise, and imbuing your daily life with mindfulness practice and calming activities.

Why must this all start with you? Why can't I just give you a checklist of changes your children should make and be done with it? Well, part of it has to do with that responsibility and modeling I've just talked about. Being the person you want your kids to become is very powerful, but it's also not easy, especially when we're facing living in such an overloaded, hectic society. There is a commonly used metaphor to illustrate this principle of starting behavior change with yourself, one I continue to use because it illustrates the idea so clearly. When you board a plane, the attendants instruct you that in the case of an emergency, you are to secure your own oxygen mask first before seeing to the needs of others. The same is true when your family is starting a downward spiral due to stress; you must take care of yourself first before you can effect any change in your kids or in your family dynamic. I understand that this goes against our normal tendency as parents, which is always to put the kids' welfare first (or to blame them first for dysfunctional family dynamics, which can be the corollary). I argue that it's not selfish to take good care of yourself or to prioritize caring for yourself and your relationship with your partner. In fact, it's a critical component to the health and well-being of your family. In case you need further convincing, allow me to make my case.

At Least We're Not Divorced . . .

Maintaining a significant relationship such as a marriage can be an arduous task (to which I'm sure my husband can attest!), and even when it's working well, a significant relationship requires careful attention and feeding. Many parents complain of feeling the closeness and intimacy they once shared with their partner start to wane as soon as their first child is born. And it's true: A little adjustment time is to be expected when a new baby comes into your life. Unfortunately, adult relationships marked by distance, stress, and anger have a significant impact on kids and families. Even when you think you're "faking it" successfully, every person in your family knows what's going on, especially your kids. Kids pick up on the fact that their parents are unhappy with each other, regardless of whether you are married or divorced, or even live in the same house.

Cognitively, kids are great perceivers of tension but poor interpreters of what's going on around them. This means that kids feel it deeply when their parents fight or are unhappy, and most often think they are responsible for the problem. The resulting effect in your kids ranges from stress and anxiety, to hostility and aggression, to depression. New studies suggest that even moderate amounts of parental conflict can wreak havoc on the lives of children, disrupting their sleep and causing negative feelings in

their day-to-day lives. Children might react to parental fights by
becoming quiet or withdrawn, or they might act out in an attempt to capture their parents' attention and keep them from
fighting with one another. With that in mind, if you improve
your parenting, you won't necessarily improve your marriage,
but if you improve your marriage, you *will* improve your parenting. Not only will you model good communication and conflict-
resolution styles and strategies, but as a happy couple you will be
more emotionally and psychologically available to your children.

It's not just about yelling. When parents give each other the
"silent treatment" in the hope their children won't notice they're
angry, kids still feel distressed. In fact, the "silent treatment" is one
of the types of fighting that has the *most* impact on kids. A three-
year study of more than three hundred families showed marked
effects on children related to adults' fighting, how they fight, and
whether they resolved their conflict in a good way. Fighting that
had the most effect on children included the silent treatment,
fights that become verbally or physically aggressive, or arguments
involving or about the children themselves. Also, contrary to the
belief parents hold, when kids are exposed to high levels of conflict between their parents, they don't get used to it. The opposite
is true: They become more sensitive and reactive to it.

This isn't to say you can't disagree with your partner ever again.
In fact, arguments and disagreements that are worked through in
a respectful and effective manner have less of an effect on kids.
Kids learn that love can last through disagreements, and that compassion and compromise go a long way toward resolving conflict.
What to do? Try to keep your major conflicts behind closed
doors, although this is not possible all the time. If you do fight,
make sure one part of the fight plays out in front of the kids:
making up! Resolving your problem in front of the children

demonstrates not only that you two are okay with one another, but also the importance of working things out when conflict arises.

Hot and Heavy Breathing

Okay, that was just to get your attention! While a warm and physically loving relationship is a great thing for the two of you, I want to move on to the second area of self-care that's critical for parents. Though I am a huge proponent of yoga and meditation, there are additional benefits that come from intense cardio exercise that you don't get from yoga or walking. Not only is it great for your body when you work a regular cardio routine into your life, it's also good for your brain, helping you stabilize your mood and stay resilient to stress.

Workouts such as bicycling, running, and even newer programs such as CrossFit and dance-based Zumba create a healthy kind of stress in the brain. This healthy stress releases serotonin, a neurotransmitter that you might remember regulates mood, appetite, and your circadian rhythms, or sleep/wake cycle. Clinically, high levels of serotonin are associated with increased happiness, while low levels are associated with depression. Though many neurotransmitters work in harmony to influence mood, serotonin is one of the most important. And like negativity, good moods are contagious. When we feel good, our kids feel good. In addition, regular exercise is great modeling for kids to encourage them to stay active and recognize the benefits of regular exercise.

Being Present

As I mentioned in the beginning of this book, the practice of mindfulness could be the single most effective way to improve your parenting, your relationships, and your health and to increase your happiness in general. Mindfulness, as I define it, is simply paying attention to the present moment without judgment. It is a particularly effective way to grow the part of your brain that registers positive emotions. In later chapters we'll go deeper into what the formal practice of mindfulness is and why it provides so many amazing benefits for kids and parents. I will introduce you to tools to develop your own practice and provide you with strategies for practicing mindfulness as a family.

Developing Resiliency

Now that we've covered some effective ways you can take care of your body and your relationships, let's move on to the next section of the book, where we'll cover what I call in my talks "sowing seeds of peace and happiness." When I talk to kids about developing their own resiliency I don't use those words, of course. Instead, I tell them that we have all different kinds of seeds in our brains. Seeds of anger, frustration, and worry are in there. We also have seeds of peace and happiness just waiting to grow.

I'll extend the metaphor for you gardeners. In a garden, the seeds that grow are the ones we nurture and pay attention to, the ones we water, and the ones we keep clear of weeds that might rob them of nutrients. Well, it is the same with our minds. Cognitively, we strengthen the neural pathways we use most frequently.

This is just another way of saying that we should pay attention to what we want to reinforce. Pay attention to the positive things in your life, and you will "reap" more positive emotions. In the chapters to come, we'll discuss great strategies and tools not only for weeding out external stress, but also for cultivating rich, positive, rewarding lives with our families.

EIGHT

The Gift of Mindfulness

In the interest of full disclosure, I've got a confession to make before we delve into this chapter on mindfulness. At first I thought it was just me, but I've since discovered that other admit to experiencing the same thing: engaging in time travel at home. Perhaps you'll discover you have done it, too.

Reading bedtime stories to young kids can be a really wonderful way to connect, share, and ease them into a sleepy place. With pillows piled high and all of us snuggled under blankets, I genuinely enjoy (most) of the reading time I've spend with my kids, even on round one hundred of some of their favorite books. As the kids got older and we didn't stop as frequently to go over words or pictures or emphasize certain sounds, it got easier. The books became more interesting to me as well, more challenging, with intriguing characters and plots that didn't just hinge on a missing cookie and a mouse. But at the same time that my extra presence was no longer required during reading time, I discovered something. I could read pages, sometimes even *chapters*, aloud, not missing a beat, while my mind reviewed my to-do list for after they fell asleep, rehashed a conversation I'd just had with my husband, or sketched out the talk I was going to give the next week. If you had asked me to repeat a single word of the page I'd just read, I wouldn't have been able to tell you. If and when I did mess up, or read a part we'd already covered, it was the kids who caught it, of course, stopping me and pulling me back to the present for a moment. But then I was off again, my body reading to my children while my mind journeyed very, very far away.

I talked to a friend about this phenomenon and she confessed she was guilty of the same crime. At first, she told me, she thought it was pretty cool that she could multitask in this way, her body automatically reading the words (though without the special voices or inflection she often brought to the reading hour) while her mind focused on another topic entirely. After that initial feeling of wonder, though, she said she felt awful. It felt more like cheating at something than like an exceptional skill that made her a multitasking mommy phenom. And the whole family was affected. Her kids noticed that she was not totally present, even if they didn't catch her every mistake. She was also missing out on some *good* stuff, the little stuff that makes up our lives—watching their faces react to the story, feeling a soft hand on her arm, noticing their eyes start to close, seeing their faces soften as they drifted toward sleep or light up with laughter at funny moments in the book.

We do it all the time, this sort of "time travel," when our bodies show up while our minds, our brains, play hooky and either jump ahead to Thursday's presentation or revisit the past. We don't do it just with our kids, but also with our spouses and even our friends. The other day a friend was telling me how excited she had been to meet up with college friends she hadn't seen in five years. She couldn't wait for the evening to arrive. However, once they were all seated around the table at the chic restaurant, she noticed she was the only one who did not have a device out on the table. Instead of reconnecting, the women were all answering distractedly while reading texts and responding to the beeps and dings that polluted the air every few minutes. Deflated, she told me she thought they would have had more intimacy if she'd stayed home and texted with them instead. Yes, we all do it, and no, it doesn't make us evil people or bad parents. It does make us disengaged instead of mindful, and harried rather than present. It also increases our stress. While your body is hanging out with your friends or your kids, you're not letting your brain get any downtime at all. Instead, it's moving a million miles a minute with your amygdala on high alert. And while you can put away the phones when you're at the table and close your computer while you help your child with homework, neither of those acts prevents your mind from disengaging, jumping frantically from one thought to the next.

The key to change is the simple but powerful act of slowing down and paying attention to one thing and remaining in the present. This is the essence of mindfulness, the practice of which I believe could be the single most effective way to improve your parenting, your relationships, and your health and well-being. Teaching your kids the practice of mindfulness can improve their ability to focus, allow them to control and regulate their emotions, manage stressful situations, and increase their happiness in general. Moreover, mindfulness does not require any particular religious training. The practice works for people of any background and any religion. Various forms of mindfulness, including the practice of yoga as a mindfulness tool, have been recommended by doctors, psychologists, and counselors as an excellent life tool for combating stress, fatigue, lack of focus, low self-esteem, and the other issues children and adults face.

It's true—I've drunk the Kool-Aid on this one! (It comprises the foundation of my work.) But if you still think mindfulness practice is too woo-woo or weird to become a part of your day-to-day life, don't just take my word for it. How about this plug for mindfulness as a core tool for living our modern American lives?

A quiet revolution is happening in America. It's not a revolution fueled by anger. It's a peaceful revolution, being led by ordinary citizens: teachers in our public schools; nurses and doctors in hectic emergency rooms, clinics, and hospitals; counselors and social workers in tough neighborhoods; military leaders in the midst of challenging conflicts; and many others across our nation. This revolution is supported by the work of scientists and researchers from some of the most prominent colleges and universities in America, such as the University of Wisconsin, Stanford, UCLA, the University of Miami, Emory, Duke, and Harvard, to name just a few . . . At the core of this revolution is mindfulness.

Congressman Tim Ryan, author of *A Mindful Nation,* wrote those words (and if anyone needs mindfulness more than parents and kids, it may very well be politicians). Ryan himself has felt the difference mindfulness has made in his life. Additionally, in his book he details the many "heroes" he found across the nation using mindfulness practice to change the lives of some of the most stressed and suffering individuals out there—from inner-city kids facing streets filled with drugs and violence to military leaders quite literally at war.

Mindfulness might be a simple idea, but it's an idea whose time has come. As we've explored in the preceding chapters, Generation Stress is at a tipping point: Today's children experience significantly more stress and pressure. Students are being diagnosed with depression, anxiety, ADHD, eating disorders, cutting, addictions, and other self-destructive behavior at epidemic rates. Cruelty, bullying, and violence are on the rise. We've seen study after study documenting the negative impact that stress is having on learning and behavior.

For many, the simple stress of living in our fast-paced, mediasaturated, multitasking world can become too much for the brain to process. In addition, many students are overwhelmed by pressure to perform and succeed. Still others cope with the stress of living in challenging, even traumatic, home environments and life circumstances that they have little power to alter in the short term. We've learned that experiencing stress changes the way their brains operate, shutting off or impairing the functioning of the prefrontal cortex, the area of the brain responsible for classroom learning. The result is kids who are significantly impaired in their ability to attend to and process information.

Mindfulness practice in general, and the program I teach, called the Mindful Life Schools method, provide children with strategies for managing stress and their emotions, no matter the circumstance, while stimulating areas of the brain related to executive functioning (the clinical term for things such as attention, problem-solving, forward thinking, impulse control, and decision making) and areas of the brain that govern empathy.

The body of evidence backs up what I experience as I travel around the country teaching mindfulness in schools. Here is a list of just some of the effects of mindfulness practice in K–12 education:

✦ Increased self-management skills and feelings of empowerment;
✦ Improvements in concentration, attention, memory, language processing, creativity, and problem-solving;

- ✦ Improvements in focus and performance;
- ✦ Increased happiness and peace of mind;
- ✦ Improvements in work habits, cooperation, attendance, and increased GPA; and
- ✦ Improvements in behavior, self-esteem, and relationship quality.

Studies and programs even report improvement in ADHD-related symptoms. What's more remarkable is that all these results come courtesy of mindfulness practice—no medication, no high-intensity training, and no religious practice or education involved.

What Exactly Do You Mean by "Mindfulness"?

You might remember my definition of mindfulness from chapter 2, but it's worth revisiting, because you'll find a lot of different characterizations of the practice out there. Before we talk about what mindfulness is, it might be helpful to talk about what it *isn't:* Mindfulness isn't texting while you "uh-huh" your kid or your partner across the dinner table. Mindfulness isn't "watching" a film on family movie night with your computer open on your lap. Mindfulness isn't walking the loop at the park while you host a virtual meeting via Bluetooth. And mindfulness isn't reading your kid a bedtime story while you revisit your argument with your sister in your head.

Instead, mindfulness, as I define it, is simply **paying attention to the present moment without judgment.** The first part of that sentence ("paying attention to the present") is pretty straightforward: paying attention to what is going on *now!*

The latter part of the sentence ("without judgment") is perhaps the most difficult and the most powerful. I love Rick Hanson's analogy of "first" and "second darts." Pain and discomfort, both mental and physical, are part of life. These uncomfortable and at times painful events are what Hanson considers to be "first darts." We can't control them, they happen to all of us, and most often we can live with them. Second darts are what get us into trouble. Second darts are our reactions to the first darts. For example, if I fail my math test, that is a first dart. The second darts might include my telling myself, *I suck at math; I am just stupid; I should have studied harder; I am a horrible student;* or blaming the teacher for making a bad test. The second darts are the judgments we cast at ourselves or at others in response to the first dart. When we are prone to second darts, as many of us are, a seemingly minor situation can turn into a catastrophe in our minds. One dart seems to be followed by another, and another. What mindfulness allows us to do is recognize the first dart, sit with it without judgment, and move forward with a thoughtful response.

I used to notice second darts often when I first learned to meditate. I would be attempting to meditate on my breathing. As always, my mind would wander. I would start to think about other things and then realize I was not meditating on my breath. My thoughts (second darts) would then turn to *I suck at this! I don't know how to meditate. Why am I so bad at this?* And so on. With mindfulness, the idea is simply to acknowledge that your mind has wandered and gently bring it back to the task at hand, in this case the breath. There is no judgment.

It's worth remembering that the formal practice of mindfulness was in a way tailor-made for Generation Stress, translated from Buddhist teachings by Jon Kabat-Zinn to combat chronic stress. Kabat-Zinn created his secular program to offer people with chronic pain and stress both relief and a reduction in symptoms. Since the inception of mindfulness, science has shown that it makes the people who practice it more self-confident, outgoing, and grateful. They have stronger immune systems; are less stressed, aggressive, anxious, or depressed; and experience fewer negative emotions in general.

While I hope you're now convinced of the effect that mindfulness can have on your life, I don't want you to overlook its importance for children. The focus of my work is teaching mindfulness skills to teachers, parents, and children. I'm consistently and genuinely astounded by the results that mindfulness has on kids and their behavior, not only in school but also at home. I spend a great deal of my time traveling between different cities and states working with teachers and parents teaching them how to bring these strategies into homes and classrooms, and we're finding that when kids learn these skills they demonstrate significant improvement in their attention, impulse control, ability to regulate their emotions, and their development of empathy. In fact, of all the work I have done with kids during the course of my career, this is by far the most effective tool for *all* kids. I have found it so effective that I have dedicated my career to traveling around the country teaching people how to do this kind of work with kids in a developmentally appropriate way.

If we take a closer look at the cognitive effects of mindfulness, it's easier to understand why the practice of it has such profound results.

What's Happening in the Brain

You know by now that whether we are consciously aware of it or not, the sounds, sensations, thoughts, and feelings of our daily life trigger neural activities within our brains at every moment. Earlier in the book I demonstrated, for example, how our computer freezing at the wrong time can trigger activation of the amygdala. Conversely, paying attention to our breathing can activate the prefrontal cortex, allowing us to slow the heart rate, lower our blood pressure, and override the alarm response set off by the amygdala. We give control back to the prefrontal cortex so higher-level thinking can occur, so we can do some real problem solving, and then we move on.

A daily mindfulness practice, comprised of an activity such as mindful breathing or mindful listening, strengthens the neural pathways in the prefrontal cortex. Instead of setting off the fight, flight, or freeze response in our amygdala, our brain makes a habit of reacting to stress and anxiety by focusing on the breath. This leads to *reflective* instead of *impulsive* responses, to greater well-being, to the ability to overcome adversity, and to an enhanced sense of peace.

The changes are not just perceived; they are physical. A Danish study from the Center of Functionally Integrative Neuroscience at Aarhus University compared MRI scans of the brains of meditators and nonmeditators. Amazingly, the MRIs showed actual physical changes in the gray matter of the lower brain stem on those who meditated. The gray matter itself was denser and bigger. This is important because the density and thickness of gray matter in a particular region of the brain are correlated with intelligence, aptitude, or skill in that area. Just as when we exercise a muscle it becomes larger and denser, in a similar way when we "exercise" our brains with meditation or mindfulness practice, we build neural mass.

Studies consistently show that people who regularly practice mindfulness demonstrate increased neural activity in the prefrontal cortex, which is correlated with increased cortical thickening in the areas related to attention. In addition, we see increased activity in the insula, or the part of your brain that supports empathy and self-awareness, and also in the left prefrontal cortex, which is associated with positive emotions.

Yet you don't need to devote your life to meditation, or become a monk, to see changes and benefits. One study showed changes in cognitive functioning after only four training sessions in mindfulness practice. Tests showed that those who had meditated demonstrated significant improvements in working memory, verbal fluency, and executive function—the smart or reasoning part of our brains.

Mindfulness practice is also an excellent way to balance the constant and automatic kickoff of your sympathetic nervous system—hello, amygdala—due to stress by arousing instead the processes of the parasympathetic nervous system (PNS), also referred to as the "rest and digest" system. The SNS and PNS are designed to work in harmony. As we know, we're tipping more and more toward overuse of our sympathetic nervous system, staying in that heightened state of reactivity. Our bodies need the PNS to pull its weight in order to provide a sense of calm and to bring our system back into balance. Actively stimulating the parasympathetic nervous system through mindfulness practice allows you to regain mindful balance, leaving you both calmer *and* more alert. This is also the reason mindfulness has been proven to help people with digestive issues and to improve sleep, because these functions are part of the PNS.

Working a mindfulness practice into yours and your kids' lives could also mean getting sick less often or, when you do get sick, healing more quickly. One study of AIDS patients showed that mindful meditation boosted immune response. Patients who engaged in formal mindfulness practice for eight weeks retained their initial levels of immune cells attacked by the virus, while those who did not engage in mindfulness showed a sharp reduction. The more mindfulness training sessions the patients attended, the higher his immune cell count at the end of the study. Though researchers don't know precisely why, they surmise that mindfulness helped control the secretion of the stress hormones adrenaline and cortisol, allowing the immune cells to remain more active. According to Harvard researchers, mindfulness also slows aging, having a neuro-protective effect on the brain. It's also good for the heart, acting to smooth heart rhythms and producing nitric oxide in the arteries, which dilates them thereby reducing blood pressure.

Over thirty years of research has shown that mindfulness de-creases stress, anxiety, depression, and hostility. It has been shown to improve both immune and executive functioning. However, all this research has been done on adults. Now researchers are turning their attention to the newly emerging discipline of mind-fulness in K–12 education, the basis of my work and that of others, actively investigating to see if mindfulness practice in children and adolescents enhances attention, executive function, and learning; and promotes pro-social behavior and general well-being, as oc-curs in adults. The initial results are encouraging.

Why Mindfulness Should Be One of Your Kid's Electives

I find it ironic that parents and teachers ask our kids to "pay at-tention!" countless times each day, but we don't take the time to teach them the skills they need to do so. The practice of mindful-ness does just that, teaching children how to pay attention to the present moment. This way of paying attention enhances both academic and social-emotional learning. The program I teach, Mindful Life Schools, combines the practices of mindfulness with movement activities to introduce children to the benefits of mindfulness in a fun and developmentally appropriate way. The movement component of the program is creative and play-based. I use engaging movement games to create a positive association in the brain with the mindfulness skills children learn. This allows them to access and utilize the skills more readily.

The mission of my work with Mindful Life is to provide children, families, and schools with brain-based mindfulness tools and strategies to help them become more resilient to the stressors in their lives. While much of this book has focused on what you can do at home to effect change, imagine the benefits if all the good things you were doing at home were also being practiced in school in developmentally appropriate ways. Another major benefit of introducing mindfulness practice in school has to do with equity. Some kids face more challenges than others, and receive less support at home. While some parents have the ability and wherewithal to engage in technology cleanses at home or to give their kids more time to play outside, other parents have much more limited resources and time, and some kids don't have a safe environment in which to engage in outside play. All children, regardless of their background, identity, or physical ability, deserve to learn the stress management skills that will help them flourish. Supporting mindfulness programs in schools gives all kids an opportunity to learn skills that they might otherwise not receive. Finally, the practice of mindfulness stimulates the prefrontal cortex, the part of the brain that is essential for classroom learning. When all children are ready to learn, classrooms simply function more effectively for everyone.

There are many programs available that focus either on mindfulness, yoga, or social-emotional learning. The program I developed and teach is theoretically derived from and informed by the latest scientific research in the fields of cognitive neuroscience, positive psychology, social and emotional learning, and mindfulness. The method was developed for use with children in pre-K through fifth grade, but can easily be adapted for older children. However, there are hosts of other programs in use in schools that also aim to introduce even the youngest children to the science of the brain. I like how Dr. Amy Saltman, cofounder and director of the Association for Mindfulness in Education, puts it. Through the practice of mindfulness in schools across the country, children can learn "how their thoughts and actions affect their brain and how their brain affects their thoughts and actions," giving them a foundation of resiliency to face everyday challenges, whether it's someone cutting in front of them at the lunch line or four hours of homework a night. Mindfulness practice in schools gives kids tools for regulating their emotions, developing better friendships, and exhibiting empathy. It gives them an understanding of how their brain works, and helps them curb their impulsive behavior and focus their attention.

Cultivating Mindful Children

We know that many schools are piling on the homework, doing away with recess, and in general drilling our students like never before—all of which results in severe consequences on kids' stress levels. While reintroducing downtime and creative play into your child's life will help alleviate that stress and pressure, so will teaching him the elements of mindfulness. Most studies track school-based programs because they are easier to evaluate, but all mindfulness programs show promising and illuminating effects. Moreover, kids are never too young, or too old, to begin to incorporate mindfulness into their lives.

I was excited to receive the results of our own study, performed in six northern Colorado preschools, to judge the effectiveness of the Mindful Life Schools (MLS) program to increase young kids' behavioral self-regulation and emotion regulation and to decrease parent and teacher stress. In the study, four- to five-year-old preschoolers received ten weekly thirty-minute sessions facilitated by their teacher. Sessions consisted of explicit mindfulness and movement activities and lessons centered on focused and open attention, impulse control, sensory awareness, emotion regulation, and empathy. In addition to the MLS groups, there were control groups of preschoolers who received no instruction, and a preschool that had integrated yoga but no material related to mindfulness and empathy.

The expected outcome of the evaluation study—what we *hoped* to find—was evidence that the MLS program, as compared to the control and yoga-only groups, contributed to:

♦ **Increased child behavioral self-regulation:** It was hypothesized that the program would increase kids' abilities to adjust their behaviors to fit different situations, such as to pay attention when they were supposed to, not to take toys away from other kids, or to motivate themselves to complete a task.

♦ **Increased child emotion regulation:** The program was expected to help kids calm strong emotions or feelings, (i.e., calm the stress response when they needed to).

- **Decreased parent stress:** The program was expected to decrease the amount of stress reported by parents of participants.
- **Decreased teacher stress:** The program was expected to decrease the amount of stress the participating children's teachers reported.

The great news is that the study confirmed all four hypotheses. The MLS program had significant, positive effects on child emotion regulation and behavioral self-regulation as well as parent and teacher stress. The program not only worked for kids who started a bit below average in these capabilities, but was also able to increase already adequate emotion regulation, behavioral self-regulation, and stress strategies, too. It made kids who were already fairly successful at self-regulation even better at it. Not only did the kids' behavior improve, but so did the stress level of the teachers involved in the program.

Although parents of the children in the MLS group did not directly participate in the program, they still reported decreased levels of parenting-related stress. Most likely this means that children who can better regulate their emotions and behaviors are more likely to make parenting easier, and thus reduce feelings of parenting-related stress. Children who participated in the MLS program were able to affect indirectly and positively their parents' stress levels. This shows that the effects of the MLS program may be able to "jump contexts," in a sense, leaving the preschool classroom and affecting the home environment as well.

The results from our study are corroborated by others. One school-based program evaluated forty-four pre-K kids who engaged in mindful awareness practices (MAPs) for thirty minutes, twice a week, for eight weeks consecutively. A control group received no mindfulness training. Teacher reports indicate the executive functioning of kids in the treatment group was positively affected, meaning they showed increased working memory and planning and organizing skills over the nontreatment group. The kids who were taught mindfulness also showed greater control of their emotions and more empathy. The good news for kids who experience problems in school is that MAP seems to have an even stronger effect on children with executive function difficulties, or those kids who have trouble controlling their emotions or who lack both focus and an ability to concentrate. These preliminary data support the introduction of mindfulness practices to pre-K children as an effective tool to improve self-regulation, particularly of "executive function" behaviors such as planning and organizing. Translation: calm, cool, capable preschoolers.

Important in today's world, mindfulness shows real promise for kids suffering from ADHD behaviors and difficulty focusing. In a randomized controlled trial conducted by Dr. Maria Napoli of Arizona State University, first-, second-, and third-graders who participated in a biweekly mindfulness and relaxation course for six weeks showed significant increases in attention and social skills and decreases in test anxiety and ADHD behaviors. A UCLA study showed similar results for second- and third-graders. Perhaps even more important, kids who started the program with emotional difficulties and trouble with focus and organization reaped the most benefit. A Stanford study showed that mindfulness worked similarly for middle-school-age kids as well.

Even (or perhaps *especially*) our technology-addled teenagers can reap the benefits of mindfulness practice, improving their outlook, functioning, and well-being. Research on teaching mindfulness to adolescents, conducted by psychologist Gina Biegel, showed teens with reduced symptoms of anxiety, depression, and physical distress. The teens had better sleep quality and increased self-esteem. Teens in the mindfulness treatment group scored better on diagnostic tests and showed significant increases in global assessment of functioning scores versus the control group. In layperson's terms, this means that adolescents who were initially diagnosed with clinical depression and anxiety were no longer depressed or anxious after mindfulness practice—a remarkable, and achievable, result.

Additional Benefits of Formal Mindfulness

Mindfulness brings tangible positive change not only to the person engaged in the practice (whether an adult or child) but also to everyone around him. Just as the parents and teachers of kids who participated in the MLS study reported decreased stress, the converse also proves true. Even if your child doesn't engage in a mindfulness program in school or at home, when parents (and teachers!) practice mindfulness it doesn't just lead to decreased stress for them, but also brings profound benefits to the kids around them. In one study, out of UCLA, parents who practiced mindfulness for one year were dramatically more satisfied with their parenting skills and their interactions with their children even though they had learned no new parenting practices. Over the course of the yearlong study, the behavior of their kids also changed. They got along better with their siblings, they were less aggressive, and their social skills improved—and all their parents had done was practice mindfulness. This is one of the reasons I strongly believe that mindfulness in families should begin with *you*. We spend so much time rehashing the past or rehearsing for the future in our minds that we can completely lose track of what's going on around us in the moment. Remember that, at its core, mindfulness is an exercise in paying attention to the here and now, something we have learned is incredibly hard to do in our culture.

While I haven't directly used the term before, the preceding chapters have all addressed what we call informal mindfulness. Think of anything you do where you feel completely engaged in the present moment. Maybe it's baking, or playing hockey, or fishing, or painting—that's informal mindfulness. Every time you are completely aware of the present moment, whether it's eating an apple, or laughing with your child, or taking a mental snapshot of a beautiful sunset—that's informal mindfulness. Taking a minute to draw a breath when you're feeling stressed is also informal mindfulness.

While those are all good things that make you feel better in the moment, practicing mindfulness formally and regularly brings that moment-to-moment awareness into our daily lives, offering us resiliency against those pressures and stressors we cannot control. Formal mindfulness practices might include sitting meditation (which I give an example of later), mindful breathing, mindful listening, and mindful eating.

Because this topic is so central to building resiliency, this chapter and the next look a little different from the preceding chapters. I've spend this chapter building a case for formal mindfulness practice. In the chapter that follows I offer step-by-step formal practice suggestions for adults, younger kids, and older kids. If you are able to, taking a class or getting help from an instructor can be incredibly beneficial. I also offer resources so you can take courses to develop your own practice or read books that will give you more self-help options.

Here's how to begin:

Developing Your Own Practice

I can't tell you how many times I hear, "Oh, I could never meditate. My mind moves way too quickly for that. It would never work." First of all, *all* our minds move too quickly. Second, if you feel this way, you are likely to receive the greatest benefits from the practice! I will tell you that no one does this perfectly. I will also warn you that it is not easy. It takes a tremendous amount of discipline and commitment to maintain a daily practice, but as I've just stated, the rewards are tremendous!

One type of formal mindfulness practice is what you might think of as "meditation." It comprises a regular time set aside to sit silently and bring your attention to your breath or to the sounds around you. In a walking meditation, you slowly walk a determined route with mindfulness to your body and your breath. With formal practice, *be* is the operative word, not *do*. Your formal practice is a time you set aside each day for mindfulness, and you practice it whether you feel stressed or not. I find that the more I practice formally, especially when I do not feel particularly stressed, the more moment-to-moment awareness I am able to exhibit.

As I've said before, informal mindfulness is encompassed by much of what we've covered in the book so far: taking time not to react, but to act with purpose; being reflective instead of reactive; being aware of your surroundings; avoiding multitasking; being present during conversations. It's good to incorporate both formal and informal mindfulness into your daily life, as the formal process strengthens those pathways in the brain and makes a mindful response your go-to reaction, while informal mindfulness keeps your day on a more even keel. Even if you still don't have a clear idea what a formal practice might look like, in the following chapter you'll learn the essential steps for a basic formal mindfulness practice that you can develop into a personalized routine, and dozens of informal games and activities that will support and enrich a practice for the entire family.

NINE

A Guide to Creating a Mindful Family

Now that we know exactly what mindfulness is, it's time to frame in concrete terms what formal mindfulness looks like. When I'm teaching this practice to kids, I make sure I touch upon at least one of the five components that, taken together, create the basics of any good mindfulness program:

1. creating space;
2. increasing awareness;
3. growing seeds of peace and happiness;
4. cultivating empathy and compassion; and
5. developing patience and persistence in the face of adversity.

We begin with **creating space**. This is a core practice consisting of noticing and using our breath and increasing our ability to become more resilient to the stress in our lives. Creating space can lead to an increase in our ability to act *reflectively* instead of *impulsively* and to respond to any given situation with forethought instead of with our first thought (which, especially if we are angry or stressed, might not be the best one).

Increasing awareness is about bringing our attention to the present moment, and staying engaged and aware. Activities that increase awareness combat our tendency to multitask, help us rein in our "time travel" when we're with our loved ones, and allow us to fully enjoy the gift of the moment.

We've talked in previous chapters about how I explain the ability to cultivate a positive mindset with kids as **growing seeds of peace and happiness,** which is just as important as **cultivating empathy and compassion** to combat negative self-talk and destructive perfectionism, increase connectedness with other people, and combat bullying behaviors.

The final and critical component of our mindfulness practice is that which helps us in **developing patience and persistence in the face of adversity.** As much as we might want to, we can't keep our kids from confronting difficult people or living in a materialistic world that often celebrates and promotes nonempathic behaviors. But adversity doesn't have to be a three-headed mythical monster; it also comes in the form of daily issues for us all, including a challenging co-worker, a spelling test, or snarled traffic.

It is important to establish a core mindfulness practice that you can commit to. (Although you may want to read through the whole chapter before putting your plan together.) I believe that we receive the most benefits from mindfulness when we dedicate a few minutes each day to a formal practice in the form of creating space. For example, I strongly encourage you to commit to a sitting meditation practice of mindful breathing for at least five minutes a day. We all can find five minute in our day, whether we have to wake up five minutes earlier, go to sleep five minutes later, or arrive five minutes early to pick up our kids and meditate in the carpool line (one of my favorites). Dedicating just five minutes a day is small change that can make a huge difference for you and your family.

In each additional section that follows, I encourage you to pick one activity that resonates with you and that you think will be a good fit for your family. After it becomes routine, you can add more or try something new. Try to use at least one practice from each section to enjoy the most comprehensive benefits.

One final note: As you read through the specific mindfulness techniques appropriate for younger kids, you may be surprised at how active some of these techniques seem. It doesn't fit with many people's vision of sitting quietly in the lotus position. This is intentional—*especially* for young children—and follows the brain-based reasoning we used in developing our in-school program.

Not only does doing Bumble Bee Breath, for example, make mindfulness fun and appealing for little kids, there is real science behind it. Learning that is connected to happy, positive emotional experience, such as learning that is playful or makes you laugh, causes the information to get stored in the long-term memory part of your brain. Conversely, learning that takes place in conditions that cause stress and anxiety is stored in short-term memory and is not available for long-term use. As we introduce the practice of mindfulness to our families, we want to make it as positive an experience as possible. I have learned that when kids create a positive experience around learning mindfulness skills, they are more likely to access those skills when they really need them. So while stillness and quiet are important and necessary, don't be afraid to get wild, play, and laugh a lot, too!

Creating Space

WHAT'S HAPPENING IN THE BRAIN

When we are in a state of stress, effective and productive thinking (the kind that takes place in the prefrontal cortex) cannot occur. A formal daily practice that includes mindful breathing meditation supports the strong function of the prefrontal cortex. It keeps the peaks associated with our stress response lower, and helps us bring our parasympathetic nervous system (PNS) and sympathetic nervous system (SNS) back into balance more quickly.

A basic sitting meditation that includes mindful breathing is a core practice and one of the best ways to prevent and manage the stress response. When we pay attention to our breathing, we slow the heart rate, lower blood pressure, and override the alarm response set off by the amygdala. In addition, when we focus on our breathing through a daily practice, it strengthens the neural pathways in the prefrontal cortex and teaches our brain to focus on the breath in response to stress, allowing us to react mindfully and reflectively, instead of impulsively or with anger or panic. The more we practice mindful breathing, the easier it becomes for us to self-regulate our emotions in this way. Mindful breathing is simple to learn, powerful, and doesn't require any special equipment. After all, we always have access to our breath!

KEY

Each activity has been coded to indicate the age for which it is appropriate. You'll see that many activities work across ages and make for good family mindfulness techniques.

Y = young children
E = elementary-age kids
T = teens
A = adults

ACTIVITIES FOR CREATING SPACE

Sitting Meditation (Mindful Breathing)   **E T A**

Sitting meditation not only improves our concentration, but also allows us to spend some time getting to know ourselves, and thus more clearly understand our thoughts, feelings, motivations, and desires. It's a great way to learn how to let go of the drama! Setting aside a special time for your practice encourages the routine and increases the effectiveness. Also, make sure you do your practice in a quiet space, away from distractions and noise. Begin with good, stable posture that will remain comfortable and won't distract you from your practice. You can sit upright in a chair with your feet flat on the floor or you may find that sitting on the floor on a cushion with your legs crossed works best. Make sure you keep your spine upright and straight. Use a cushion if you need to, in order encourage good posture. Keep your arms loose and at your sides. Don't clench your fists or hands. Keep your chin down. You may close your eyes, which is sometimes easier for beginners, or let them softly focus on a given point. Stay still.

In sitting meditation, the first step is to become aware of your breathing. Don't try to alter it; just bring your awareness to it. Try to stay present with your breathing as air goes in and then while you exhale. Notice how your breath changes, the differences in the length or depth of your breath, and notice whatever thoughts or feelings come to you while you breathe. As you continue, you will notice that you begin breathing with your belly instead of shallowly, in your chest. People can feel self-conscious about letting their bellies stick out, but this is the kind of breathing we want to engage in, and no one is there to see you! Let your hand rest on your belly and feel your breath as it flows in and out of your body.

If your mind wanders (which it will, time and time again) simply notice that your mind has wandered and bring your awareness back to your breath. If you find yourself thinking of something stressful, you will notice a shift in your breath. If this happens, take a few deep breaths, with long exhalations, until your regulate yourself and return to deep-belly breathing and focus. Overall, the goal is not to change how you breathe, but instead to notice that you are breathing.

In the beginning, try to do this practice for five minutes at the start or end of the day. Then work your way up to both, or try to increase your sitting time to twenty minutes, if you are able. Even if you stick to five minutes a day, this small amount of formal practice will make a difference in how you manage your stress, in your overall well-being, and, though you can't see it, in your brain!

Meditating with Your Kids　　　Ⓥ Ⓔ Ⓣ Ⓐ

It can be fun to share sitting meditation with your kids. First, it must be something they are interested in trying. Meditation loses all effectiveness when someone is forced to do it! I started practice with my daughter when she was seven. It worked best for us to make it part of the bedtime routine. In her room, we kept a singing bowl, some candles, and special pillows, which we used as meditation cushions. I explained to her what a mindful body looked like—sitting cross-legged, spine straight, with hands resting in your lap. As part of our routine we would light the candles, and I would let her decide whether she wanted to practice mindful breathing or mindful listening (bringing focused awareness to the sounds you hear). I also let her choose the amount of time (usually between three and five minutes). I have an app on my phone that allows you to set a timer; a nice chime rings when the time is up. My daughter is in charge of setting the timer. Some nights she is very still and focused; on others she is more restless, and that is okay. Part of the benefit for her is simply observing me as I meditate. It has been a wonderful addition to our nightly routine. While it is great to meditate with your children, it is critical to dedicate a separate time for your own practice.

Bottle Breathing　　　Ⓥ Ⓔ Ⓣ Ⓐ

In classrooms, I like to teach kids the technique of bottle breathing. Using an empty bottle, show your child what happens when you pour water into the bottle. The bottom of the bottle fills first. As you keep pouring, the water gets higher and higher until it reaches the top. When you pour the water out, the water empties first from the top. Add food coloring to the water and say the "magical liquid" left in the bottle is just like the air we breathe. Pretend the bottle sits in our bodies, with the bottom part of the bottle in our bellies and the neck of the bottle rises up through your chest and neck. Tell your kids that when they breathe in, the air goes first to the bottom of the bottle, and the magical liquid grabs all the bad feelings. Then the bad feelings leave their body with the air they exhale. As kids get older, we will speak more about sitting *with* feelings and not trying to change them, but when children are young this can be a helpful metaphor for teaching them about the power of their breath.

Animal Breathing Ⓥ Ⓔ

Teach your kids the importance of breath and breathing by having them breathe in the form of various animals. This is the Bumble Bee Breath exercise I alluded to earlier. It's a great technique for young kids. It uses fun to teach them about mindful breathing and gets their imaginations going. You can incorporate the breathing into bedtime stories about animals, or just encourage them to breath like a lion or a snake to help calm themselves as they try to fall asleep. I dare you not to enjoy doing this one with them!

Some of my favorites include Bumble Bee Breath, where you inhale through the nose, then exhale with lips together to make a humming sound. It can be fun to sit cross-legged and back to back to try this exercise. You can feel the vibration from the other person and this often triggers laughter! Snake Breath is an inhalation through the nose followed by (what else?) an exhaled *hissssss* with teeth together. This one is great for cooling down hot tempers. Or try the Lion Breath, also good for managing anger. Inhale through the nose, then exhale through the mouth with your tongue hanging out. For a balancing breath, do as a bear does. Inhale through the nose while counting to three (inside your head or on your fingers). Exhale through the nose for five counts. The reason this works is that when we are in the midst of a stress response, our inhalation is longer than our exhalation; increasing the time we take to exhale brings the sympathetic and parasympathetic nervous systems back into balance.

Creating Mindful Habits   T A

We live in a world of instant gratification, and it's no wonder children become used to this, and often struggle to learn patience. Using mindfulness practice in this way can help us all develop patience.

Look for opportunities throughout your day to bring your awareness to your breath. For example, take three to five mindful breaths before you answer the phone, when you find yourself stuck in traffic, when you are placed on hold, or when you are waiting in line.

Relax Your Tongue and Jaw   E T A

When we are stressed we often hold tension in our mouths, clenching our jaws and grinding our teeth. The intentional relaxation of our mouths allows the rest of our bodies and our minds to calm.

Touch Your Lips   (E) (T) (A)

It may sound weird, but your PSN is triggered by the mere touch of fibers spread throughout our lips. (Maybe that's why we enjoy kissing so much!) Lightly touching your lips (especially combined with deep breathing) prompts your body to activate the PNS and evokes a feeling of calm.

Slow Down   (T) (A)

Notice if you're talking quickly on the phone, typing ninety words a minute on your computer, or zipping in and out of traffic—and simply slow down. Notice if you are jiggling your leg impatiently or tapping a pencil on the table. Stop the restless movement and enjoy doing things more slowly and feeling calmer.

Stop Multitasking   (T) (A)

Do one activity at a time and do it well. Instead of multitasking, allow yourself the pleasure of focusing on one activity, whether that's helping your kids with homework, writing a report, or unloading the dishwasher.

Visualization   (V) (E) (T) (A)

If you notice you are feeling anxious or nervous, visualize a safe or pleasant and carefree place. It could be a treasured site from childhood, a favorite vacation spot, or even an exotic locale. Try to imagine and then feel your environment, vividly projecting yourself in that space—calm and serene. Young children can use guided relaxation such as stories found on the Mindful Life Dreamzzz CD or from a story you tell them to help them with visualization.

Increasing Awareness

What's Happening in the Brain

You know by now that when the brain is in a stressful state this has a significant impact on not only our general well-being but also our success in learning and working. While we often think of "pouring it on" when we really want to get something done, in reality, the opposite tack is more successful. True focus, engagement, competency, and achievement are possible only when our brains are in a calm, receptive state.

The following awareness activities give us the opportunity to be both calm *and* focused. These fun and engaging exercises feed our natural childlike curiosity, providing a relaxed yet alert state of mind. They give us the opportunity to practice paying attention to the present moment, which helps us absorb details and think clearly. The more opportunity we have to formally practice this type of mindful attention, the easier it becomes for us to use it successfully in our day-to-day experiences, whether that involves my teen taking a math test or my focusing on writing. Activities such as mindful listening, listening to the present sounds, and paying attention strengthen the reticular activating system (RAS). This is the part of the brain that helps us filter out distracting stimuli and focus our attention.

ACTIVITIES FOR INCREASING AWARENESS

Mindful Listening   Ⓥ Ⓔ Ⓣ Ⓐ

A tone bar bought from a music store or online is a great tool for both adults and kids, as long as you are mindful that it is to be used to reduce stress, not to punish or force attention. Purchase an inexpensive tone bar from a music store, or buy a Buddhist-style prayer bowl. Each works similarly in that if you strike the tone bar or circle around the prayer bowl's rim, it will emit an extended note. (A tone bar has no religious association, if that matters to you.)

Sit cross-legged, and have your kids sit cross-legged near you and close their eyes. Strike the tone bar and have them listen to the sound of the tone. Tell them to raise their hand when the sound stops for them. This keeps their awareness focused on the sound alone. This type of mindful listening strengthens the neural pathways in the prefrontal cortex and is a great "focusing" exercise that can help calm your child and get her prepared for homework, dinnertime, or a change in activity.

Another option is to go outside (if you live somewhere with nature sounds) or play a nature CD. You can even download an app with nature sounds. Have kids listen carefully to what they hear and try to identify the source of the sounds. There are no wrong answers; it's the careful listening that is important.

If you are on a walk or a hike, even on the way to school, stop and listen for a minute with your eyes closed. Have everyone share what they've heard.

As a variation on listening to nature sounds, try listening to a song and have your child identify different instruments: bass, drums, guitar, etc.

Noticing the Present Moment   Ⓥ Ⓔ Ⓣ Ⓐ

While walking with or driving your kids to school, have them look for things that are new, unusual, or things they simply have not noticed before along the route. Identify weather patterns, the shifting seasons, or stop to notice the sun playing across water, trees beginning to leaf, or the changing color of the seasons.

Mindfulness Through Play   Ⓥ Ⓔ

For preschoolers, some of the most fun ways to teach awareness is through some very classic games. Red Light, Green Light may elicit a lot of giggles, but it also requires a great amount of focus for preschoolers to do well. To play, color a piece of paper green on one side and red on another. A leader stands facing the kids a small distance away. Kids start in an even line. When the paper is turned green side out, the kids advance toward the leader. When the paper is flipped red side out, the kids must stop immediately. Kids who don't stop return to the start and begin again. Keep turning the paper, stopping and starting, until one child reaches the leader and becomes the leader. If you don't want to use a piece of paper, the leader can also turn her back to the group when the light is "green" and turn to face the group when the light is "red." Simon Says taps the same kind of focus.

Tree Pose

A wonderful balance pose that is good for all ages, the tree pose offers an additional benefit: it is impossible to be a good tree without your body coming to a complete stop and being fully at rest. Stand in an upright posture, with your feet slightly apart, arms at your sides, feeling the weight of your body evenly distributed between both legs. Press the soles of your feet into the floor. Slowly shift your weight onto your right leg. Raise your left leg, bending it at the knee, and bring the sole of your foot to rest against your right leg just below the knee or against your inner thigh, if you are able. Keep both hips squared to the front. Bring your palms together in front of your chest. Balance on your right leg, feeling the strength of your connection and grounding yourself into the floor. Relax and breathe.

You can alter this game and play 1-2-3 Mindful Tree. Here's how to play: A group of kids (or even your family) lines up on one end of a field or large room. One person faces away from the group at the other end and says, "One, two, and three . . ." as everyone in the group moves toward the person counting. After the counter says "three," he waits and then yells out, "Tree!" prompting everyone to freeze where they are in the tree pose. The objective is to reach the counter; the first one to do so becomes the counter, and you start again. To slow things down, decide before the counter begins that the group will move in the manner of an animal such as a crab (doing a crab walk), a bear, a snake, an eagle, a dog, etc.

Use Your Nondominant Hand   (E) (T) (A)

Your dominant hand is the hand you use to throw a ball or write your name. As anyone who's ever had a broken arm or hand can tell you, switching to your nondominant hand, even for simple tasks, requires a great deal of concentration! While fairly rudimentary, this task requires focused attention and awareness in the present moment. Most of us can write our names or feed ourselves without conscious will of what our hand is doing. Here we are forced to be present and engaged.

Try eating with your nondominant hand as a family. (Forks are easiest—don't try soup right off the bat.) Or have your kids use their nondominant hand to write their name at the top of their homework, being as neat as they can. Experiment with other activities and see what you discover. For some reason, I throw a Frisbee *better* with my nondominant hand. Are their certain activities that your family members can do easily or better with the other hand or foot?

Mindful Driving   (T) (A)

In the age of cell phones this is an important activity for everyone, but it's especially great for teens, who might get easily distracted on the road. Still, it's not just kids who do this. How many of us have arrived at work and thought, "How did I get here?" or have tried to drive to one destination and found ourselves driving somewhere else, to our kids' school or to work instead? Drives we do every day can become something we do completely on autopilot. Instead, use your commute as an opportunity to practice mindfulness. Notice how long you actually sit at a light that seems to stay red forever. What changes do you notice along your route? Try an alternative route to school or work. Notice how many right turns or left turns you take as part of your commute. Observe your commute with all of your senses.

Become Mindful of Your Speech   E T A

It's a very interesting exercise to try to eliminate filler words from your speech. For example, it used to drive my husband and me crazy when our daughter added the word *like* to every sentence. Then, when I tried this exercise, I realized that I was using the word *basically* basically all the time! You can even turn this into a game similar to Slug Bug (without the hitting), in which family members gently remind us when we mindlessly pepper our speech with filler words.

Eat Mindfully   Y E T A

Not only does eating mindfully enhance our enjoyment of food and increase our gratitude for having food, but taking the time to eat mindfully allows us to eat less, signals us when we're full, and improves our overall digestion. Kids especially tend to eat well when they start the meal with mindful eating.

Begin by taking one minute at meal time to eat mindfully. Don't talk. Instead, simply notice the smell, texture, look, and feel of the food in your mouth. I limit it only to a minute, because we also want our meals to be a time to engage with each other. Starting a dinner or even our rushed morning meals with a moment of silence can help everyone center themselves and bring the present moment to our enjoyment of our food.

Notice What's Around You　　　　　Ⓔ Ⓣ Ⓐ

Pick an object in your environment that you are going to be intentional in noticing. You can choose any object, though, for starters trees are wonderful to notice. Pay attention to all the different types, colors, leaves, bark textures, and smells of the trees around you. Other fun things to notice are spiderwebs, clouds, stars, flowers, buildings, or even certain kinds of houses. Once, when we were in Portland, I pointed out to my kids how many brick Tudor-style homes were in my sister's neighborhood. My son had us all laughing as he took joy in screaming, "Tooter!" every time we passed one.

Smile and Nod　　　　　Ⓥ Ⓐ

In this practice, pay attention to and notice your impulse to disagree. People are always going to say things we don't agree with. The next time a controversial topic arises, challenge yourself to remain quiet. This works well for adults talking about politics and can be great practice for siblings who are in a terrible bickering phase. When you resist the urge to argue, notice if the outcome of the conversation is different. Did your compliance or lack of resistance change the conversation? Were there times when you remained quiet when you felt like speaking? Especially for kids, this can open a wonderful discussion of when it is important to speak up and when it might be better just to smile and nod.

Even when we agree or are interested in what others are saying, sometimes we spend less time listening than we do planning our response or framing what we will say when it's our turn to talk. The next time you go to a social event or even talk with a friend, be intentional about mindfully listening to others as they speak. Try to fully listen and then respond, rather than thinking about what your response is going to be before the person has finished speaking.

Notice Your Favorite Color   Ⓨ Ⓔ Ⓣ Ⓐ

Have one of your kids pick a color at the beginning of the day and notice how many things they see over the course of the day that are that color. They can write them down if it helps them keep track. Talk about your findings over dinner.

Mindful Hike   Ⓔ Ⓣ Ⓐ

If you take a walk through a park or along a tree-lined street, spend five minutes on mindful listening, five minutes on mindful seeing, and five minutes on mindful smelling. What did you notice?

Leave No Trace   Ⓔ Ⓣ Ⓐ

Some people say a cluttered environment creates a cluttered mind, and for me that's definitely true! I got this idea from a book called *How to Train a Wild Elephant and Other Adventures in Mindfulness,* and I've adapted it here for families.

In Leave No Trace, each family member chooses one room of the house that is regularly used. For one week, each time that person enters his chosen room, he tries to leave no trace that he was there—no stray papers, no dishes, no toys or shoes or coats or bags. If anyone else enters one of these rooms over the course of the week, it is their responsibility to clean up in such a way that leaves no trace, or any clue that they have been there.

It is helpful to put a sign on the door of the room (or in a prominent place if the room has no door) that reads, LEAVE NO TRACE, to remind family members of the game. This task helps family members become aware of their tendency to turn away from certain tasks they're reluctant to do, all those small things that we could take care of during the day but somehow don't have the motivation for.

To truly leave no trace we have to be mindful of our environment. We need to pay attention to discrete tasks and make sure they are done properly. The exercise also combats the tendency toward procrastination or laziness, and eliminates nagging about cleaning up toys, books, papers, shoes, or backpacks.

Body Scan   E T A

Use "imagination breathing" to do your own body scan. Have your child lie down, close her eyes, and take a deep breath in and out through her mouth. Then have her take a deep breath through her nose. Now is when the imagination comes in: Have her take a deep breath through her feet. Take a deep breath through the belly, heart, neck/throat, nose, and the top of her head. This is also a wonderful relaxer if you're feeling tense before bed, or need a moment before getting up to set your intention and begin your day mindfully.

Dance Party Ⓥ Ⓔ Ⓣ Ⓐ

It's not a metaphor; it's exactly what it sounds like. Turn down the lights, crank up the tunes, and have a dance party. It's great exercise: it makes us laugh, and has an added benefit in that we are typically present when we are dancing.

Mindful Shower Ⓣ Ⓐ

Remember how long you could spend in a soapy bath as a child? You noticed the water, the bubbles, the feel of the washcloth, the tile around the tub. As adults, we often take showers as quickly as possible in order to get out the door on time. Instead of rushing through a shower, your thoughts focused on your to-do list, feel the temperature of the water, smell the soap, listen to the sound of the spray. You can even try plugging your ears and listening to the difference in the sounds.

Develop a Signature Awareness Exercise Ⓣ Ⓐ

Older kids and teens like to be led toward solutions, rather than having them suggested to them. For teens, help them focus their own calming response by asking what types of activities already make them feel relaxed. Some answers my nephews and their friends have given include playing basketball, baking cookies, making playlists, hula-hooping, or even taking a hot shower. Encourage teens to take a break and engage in their own signature awareness exercises when things get stressful.

Star Gaze   Ⓥ Ⓔ Ⓣ Ⓐ

This task is easier to do away from the bright lights of the city, but even in an urban environment you can see a few stars at night. Take a moment to really notice them—their vastness, their brightness. You can appreciate the moon in the same way.

Reframe Your Day   Ⓐ

Too often when we're asked how we are, our go-to answer is "busy!" The next time you're asked, stay mindful, and help influence the mindfulness of others, by refraining from using the *B*-word. Instead, try to think of something positive going on with your or your family and talk about that instead.

Growing Seeds of Peace and Happiness

WHAT'S HAPPENING IN THE BRAIN

Our brain is three to five times more sensitive to negative information than it is to positive. This mechanism helped humans survive as we evolved—for example, it was more important to be aware of poisonous snakes than to stop and smell the beautiful flowers. Today, we don't have the same threats to our survival, yet our brains are still built to pay more attention to negative inputs than to positive.

When we intentionally pay attention to the positive things in our lives, and to positive stimuli, we strengthen the neural pathways associated with those positive memories. The more frequently those pathways are used, the more our brains opt to use them, increasing positive thoughts and lessening our focus on negative experiences.

One way to increase our attention to positive events is to practice gratitude. In addition to making us feel better, the regular practice of gratitude has been shown to help students use their prefrontal cortex (PFC), the "thinking brain," more effectively. Feeling grateful can trigger the release of dopamine to the PFC. Dopamine increases alertness, determination, attentiveness, and energy. Additionally, studies have shown that people who regularly practice gratitude

+ feel 25 percent happier;
+ are more likely to be kind and helpful to others;
+ are healthier, more enthusiastic, interested, and determined; and
+ sleep better.

Grateful children and teens tend to thrive. Kids who practice gratitude get higher grades, are more satisfied with their lives, do better socially, and show fewer signs of depression.

ACTIVITIES FOR GROWING SEEDS OF PEACE AND HAPPINESS

Express Your Appreciation   Ⓥ Ⓔ Ⓣ Ⓐ

In my house we started this as a birthday tradition. On the eve of someone's birthday, we go around the table and express what we all appreciate about that person.

Make a Gratitude Jar   Y E

This can be a fun project for kids. Find a container and let the
kids decorate it. Cut out some pieces of scratch paper and put
them in a convenient place so that family members can write
down things they feel grateful for and place the paper in the jar. If
your kids can't yet write, have them draw a picture of an item
that triggers the memory. Then open the jar once a week or once
a month and read what everyone has written.

Keep a Gratitude Journal   E T A

This is great for adults and kids, either incorporated into a regular
journaling practice or done during time set aside. This makes a
wonderful shift from how many of us keep journals or how kids
keep diaries, writing in them only when we are angry, confused,
or sad.

Who Was a Good Friend to You Today?   E T A

Instead of talking about only what went wrong during the day,
take a moment to talk with your child about who was a good
friend to them today. What did that friend do that made your
child feel good? Did your child let that friend know he helped her
or made her feel better? What feelings did that friend's generosity
of spirit inspire in your child?

The Praise Pancake   Ⓥ Ⓔ Ⓣ Ⓐ

This exercise allows us time and space to let the good sink in. Since our brains are more focused on and sensitive to negative information, we often let good experiences or compliments pass us by like water off a duck's back. So take a moment to let the good sink in. Before bed, have your child list three good things that happened to him that day. Then have him imagine he is a pancake lying there and that the good experiences are the syrup sinking in. See if he can notice sensations in his body as he does this. The only downside is that it might make him hungry!

For adults, the next time someone pays you a compliment, don't pass it off with a self-deprecating remark. Whether it's another parent praising your cupcakes at the school bake sale or a co-worker thanking you for helping her with a task, feel the power of allowing the compliment to wash over you instead of immediately deflecting it or playing it down.

Take a Mental Health Day   Ⓥ Ⓔ Ⓣ Ⓐ

Great for kids and adults! There will always be lacrosse practice, and grocery shopping to do, and homework, and a dog that needs walking, and laundry, and bills to pay. The list goes on. Once in a while the most powerful anecdote to it all is to declare a mental health day. Stay in your pajamas all day if you like. Put off the chores and enjoy one another's company instead. Play a game of football or tag. Play card games. Let the dishes wait and read a novel, or go for a bike ride. You'll feel refreshed and inspired.

Celebrate Beauty   Ⓥ Ⓔ Ⓣ Ⓐ

Whether it is the *Mona Lisa* or a mountain vista, we are surrounded by beautiful things: ornate buildings, stars, sunsets, cute babies, changing leaves. Look for beautiful things in your day.

Visualize Success   Ⓔ Ⓣ Ⓐ

To help your teen with difficult homework or a big test, have her visualize success. Ask her to imagine completing the assignment with ease, or have her visualize finishing the test with time to spare. Visualizing an experience strengthens the neural pathways associated with that experience. It works well for sports, too.

My Favorite Things   Ⓔ Ⓣ Ⓐ

Ask your child what he already does that makes him happy, anything that makes the time seem to float by. Have him make a list. Not only can your child turn to that list for informal mindfulness practice ideas, but the list itself can help pull a moody child out of a self-judgmental slump.

Do What *Feels* Good   Ⓣ Ⓐ

I love crawling into a bed made with freshly laundered sheets. A friend of mine keeps fresh flowers in her house and on her desk at all times. Be intentional about surrounding yourself with things that bring you pleasure. Clean sheets, the smell of lavender or cinnamon, freshly cut flowers—what do your kids love?

Acknowledge Your Strengths   **E** **T** **A**

If asked to make a list of five things about yourself you'd like to change most, people crank a list out pretty quickly. But when asked to list our strengths, most of us find that a bit more challenging. Make a list of your strengths. Ask people close to you what they think your strengths are. Keep the list in an accessible place, such as the front page of your journal. Look at it often. Turn to it in times when you're beating yourself up. It might help you recognize that a behavior or trait which you're critical of is actually one that others find inspiring.

Visualize Strength   **E** **T** **A**

Think about a time when you felt particularly strong. When things feel difficult, use your memory of that experience as an anchor. Close your eyes and imagine the experience. What did it look, feel, and smell like? How can you recreate that strength in this new moment?

Don't Sweat the Small Stuff   **T** **A**

Focus on only what you can control. This might come as a blow to the ego, but there is only so much in life we have power over. We can't control it when the other team plays a little better and wins the game, or when the other guy gets picked for the job. Focus on your role, perform to the best of your ability, and let go of the rest.

A New Kind of News   Ⓔ Ⓣ Ⓐ

Our brains are three to five times more sensitive to negative information than to positive. This is a leftover survival mechanism that helped humans as we evolved. You know how dispiriting it can be to watch the five o'clock news—nothing but crime and chaos! Children, too, are surrounded by stories and events that strengthen the fight, flight, or freeze response, especially kids in the tween years, who are old enough to understand the gravity of the stories while feeling powerless to take action.

Take time once a week to search the Internet or newspaper for inspiring and hopeful stories. If your children are old enough, they can participate in the search. Take turns sharing these stories once a week, over a family dinner. When we intentionally pay attention to the positive things in our life, we strengthen the neural pathways associated with those positive memories, increasing positive thoughts and lessening our focus on negative experiences. This is a great way to put into perspective the little things that bother us, and can change everyone's outlook for the better.

Cultivating Empathy and Compassion

WHAT'S HAPPENING IN THE BRAIN

Children learn empathy through face-to-face interactions. This begins when they are infants, learning that when they smile,

Mom smiles. The skill of learning empathy continues to develop through face-to-face interactions as they grow. The rise of technology, however, has led to a significant decrease in face-to-face interactions. Most children would prefer to play with a parent's phone than engage in a face-to-face conversation.

When children have repeated eye contact with a peer, they begin to recognize her as a person with feelings. When they can begin to learn this perspective, it decreases their desire bully or be unkind to other kids. Games such as Nice to Meet You and Mirroring help children become comfortable with face-to-face interactions and eye contact in a nonthreatening way, indirectly helping them develop skills of empathy. As children practice mindful seeing, they strengthen the neural pathways in the prefrontal cortex and become increasingly attuned to observing details by slowing down and focusing their attention.

When children practice acts of kindness it strengthens the neural networks in their brain that help them develop compassion and empathy. The more they practice acts of kindness, the easier it becomes for them to recognize when people are in need. Brain research demonstrates that people who practice acts of kindness and compassion are better at recognizing and identifying emotions in others, a key component to the development of empathy.

Dopamine is one of the neurotransmitters in the brain that influences our emotional states. It is also the neurotransmitter most directly associated with pleasure, attention, reward, and motivation. Studies show that, during acts of kindness, our brains are rewarded by a release of dopamine. In addition, practicing compassion builds the social and emotional competence that children need to become confident and resilient.

ACTIVITIES FOR CULTIVATING
COMPASSION AND EMPATHY

Befriend Your Body   (T) (A)

This is a favorite activity of mine from psychologist and author Dr. Rick Hansen, one I find particularly effective. Think of your body as another person, such as a good friend or a family member. If your body were a friend or family member, would you treat it differently from how you do now? Would you make it run when its knees hurt? Would you feed it only junk food? Would you keep it awake when it needed to rest? Often we treat ourselves worse than we would treat anyone else, even a stranger! Take time to be aware of how you are treating your body and let self-compassion, not judgment, guide your actions.

The Three-Breath Hug   (Y) (E)

The next time your little one has a meltdown—I mean one of those where she just can't stop sobbing—try the Three-Breath Hug. It is as simple as it sounds. Hug her closely and take three deep breaths in unison. This helps teach children how to calm themselves, it calms the stress response, and it feels great for you, too!

Give Compliments   (Y) (E) (T) (A)

For one week go out of your way to give someone a genuine compliment once a day. Model for your children the difference between a meaningful compliment related to behavior ("I appreciate that you wake up early every morning and make me coffee!") versus more materialistic compliments that don't really reflect on the person ("I like your shirt"). Have each member of the family write down the compliments they gave. At the end of the week discuss what you said and how it made you feel.

Detective Listening   Ⓔ Ⓣ Ⓐ

Listen carefully to people when they speak, almost as if you were a detective looking for clues. Try to absorb their every word. See if you can refrain from letting your thoughts wander to what *you* want to say and just listen. Notice not only their speech, but also their facial expressions and body language. How does this type of listening change your interaction with this person?

Pay It Forward   Ⓔ Ⓣ Ⓐ

Think of someone in your life who could use a little support, love, good energy. This could be a co-worker, classmate, grandparent, or friend. Go out of your way to brighten her day. Bring her a flower, write her a card, or tell her how you feel about her.

Nice to Meet You   Ⓥ Ⓔ Ⓣ

Teach your children that when they meet someone new, they should extend their hand, look the person in the eye, shake his hand, and say, "Nice to meet you!" Ensure the eye contact part by asking your kids to notice the eye color of every new person they meet and describe it to you afterward. This makes learning eye contact fun and enjoyable while cultivating empathic habits.

Mirror, Mirror   Ⓥ Ⓔ Ⓣ

This great game requires focused concentration to play. Two people stand facing each other, looking into each other's eyes. One is the leader, and the other is the "mirror." A third participant watches the two. The goal is for the "mirror" to mimic whatever physical movements the leader makes so accurately that the person watching can't tell who is the leader and who is the mirror.

Use Good Manners   Ⓥ Ⓔ Ⓣ

Be mindful of your speech. Studies show that one of the biggest influences parents have on their kids is in modeling how to treat other people. When addressing other people, be sure to be clear, compassionate, and kind, using those good old standards like "Please," "Thank you," and "Excuse me."

Be intentional in teaching and talking to your kids about manners. Ask them to wait patiently until you finish an adult conversation before interrupting. Teach them how to order their own food in restaurants, looking the server in the eye and using nice words. When adults greet them or ask them how they are, have them return the greeting and ask the adult how she is doing in return.

Developing Patience and Persistence in the Face of Adversity

WHAT'S HAPPENING IN THE BRAIN

Studies show that people who engage in process-oriented rather than outcome-oriented thinking are more resilient to adversity and challenge, are less judgmental of themselves and others, and don't fall into the terrible trap of perfectionism, in which no one wins. We can help shape a process-oriented mind-set in ourselves and our kids by using mindful praise and helping our kids set process-oriented goals, both of which will be discussed in greater detail in the next chapter.

Mindful praise takes into account a child's effort, acknowledging their willingness to attack a problem from many angles rather than focusing only on the outcome or on what they got right. Mindful communication takes into account the interests and passions of your child and uses that as a basis for increasing his motivation and willingness. Studies consistently show that people with inner motivation are those who ultimately succeed, while those provided with external motivation for doing well ("If you get an A on your test I'll buy you a video game") can't sustain their performance over the long term. In fact, they end up doing worse than kids who were never "incentivized" in that same way.

Instead of doing your child's homework for him so he doesn't ever have to face a B, or becoming that rabid parent on the sidelines telling your kid to "crush the other team," channel that fierce need to protect your child, and your wish for her to taste success, into teaching her how to manage and persist through adversity. That is the greatest gift you can give her.

ACTIVITIES FOR DEVELOPING PATIENCE AND PERSISTENCE IN THE FACE OF ADVERSITY

Become Part of a Larger Community   Ⓣ Ⓐ

Strengthen your own support network and give your kids more opportunities for high-quality connections with other kids and adults by becoming part of a larger community. This could be school- or sports-related, be a cultural or spiritual group, or involve doing service for others, such as working in your community or volunteering. This type of community involvement helps develop a shared sense of self and gives individuals strength from which to draw.

Acknowledge Mistakes   Ⓥ Ⓔ Ⓣ Ⓐ

Children develop resilience when they see their parents admit to mistakes and understand that each is an opportunity for growth and learning. At dinner, go around the table and have everyone answer the questions "What mistake did you learn from today?" This phrasing keeps the discussion learning-focused instead of directing blame and judgment.

Set Short-Term Goals   Ⓥ Ⓔ Ⓣ Ⓐ

Override that feeling of being overwhelmed by a project or goal by focusing on one task at a time and setting short-term, achievable goals. For young kids this might mean your saying to them,

"Put your blocks in the basket when you're through with them" rather than "Clean up your room and tidy your closet." For you, it might mean feeling satisfied with only having bought the kids new rain boots for fall (even though your to-do list also included doing laundry, going grocery shopping, and cleaning out the kids' closets) or with having returned only one client phone call even though three more are waiting. Acknowledge the small successes.

Teach and Model Patience   Ⓔ Ⓣ Ⓐ

We all have moments throughout the day that try our patience. Notice when you find yourself becoming impatient, notice what happens inside your body and the thoughts that race through your mind. Can you look at this time as an opportunity of some kind? Can you turn it into an opportunity to notice your environment, to take a few mindful breaths, to reflect on your day? Can you come up with strategy to ease your impatience when it arises?

Once you have more clarity, try to reframe those events that make you impatient. If you find yourself stuck in traffic or placed on hold, use the time as an opportunity to practice mindful seeing or listening, or to bring awareness to your breath. What good can you find in this moment? Model this behavior explicitly for your kids. If you're stuck in traffic with your child, for example, instead of ranting about the work being done on the freeway, say, "Oh good, now I have a chance to catch up with you about your day!"

Model Mindful Breathing   Ⓐ

When we find ourselves in a state of stress, we aren't capable of rational thinking, the kind that occurs in the prefrontal cortex. While formal mindfulness with attention to the breath encourages our brains to respond with belly breathing, we can always spur it along in the moment by using it to combat frustration or a sense of being overwhelmed. When you find yourself overwhelmed or frustrated by a situation, soothe yourself and, at the same time, set a good example by modeling deep breathing as a calming behavior for your child. Say, "I'm feeling really frustrated by this, so I am going to take a few deep breaths."

Additional Resources

Many of the suggestions just listed draw from the work of great people in my field, or are techniques I picked up from parents and teachers I've worked with over the course of my career. Others I adapted for use with families from some of the resources I list here. If you find yourself loving these techniques and want more practice, check out some of my go-to books and sites:

BOOKS

Just One Thing, by Rick Hanson
Buddha's Brain, by Rick Hanson
Coming to Our Senses, by Jon Kabat-Zinn
A Mindfulness-Based Stress Reduction Workbook,
    by Elisha Goldstein

One-Minute Mindfulness, by Donald Altman
How to Train a Wild Elephant: And Other Adventures in Mindfulness, by Jan Chozen Bays
Mindset: How We Can Learn to Fulfill Our Potential by Carol S. Dweck

BOOKS FOR KIDS

Peaceful Piggy Meditation
Moody Cow Meditates
Ahn's Anger
Each Breath a Smile
Beau the Bee
The Three Questions
Zen Shorts
The Little Engine That Could
HUG

CLASSES

In some ways, I think it is ideal to take a class in person. Search online for "MBSR courses" in your area, and you should find some options. You can also take classes online. Here are some you can check out:

For adults

Mindful Awareness Practices Through UCLA
The Tergar Learning Community. This has more of a
    Buddhist influence but provides the best introduction to

meditation that I have experienced. What is even better
is it's free! (http://learning.tergar.org/course_library/intro
-to-meditation/)

For kids

Mindful Life Schools (www.mindfullifeschools.com)
Inner Kids (http://www.susankaisergreenland.com)
Stressed Teens (http://www.stressedteens.com/about-2/stressed
   -teens/)
Mindful Schools (http://www.mindfulschools.org)

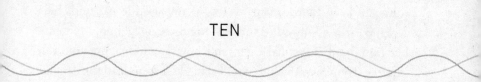

TEN

What a Little Face Time Can Do

Last year I took a magical vacation to Costa Rica with my family. We spent ten days, just the four of us. No playdates, no TVs, no cell phones or computers to distract us from each other. We enjoyed the tangle of verdant jungle around us and the pleasure of one another's company. It was amazing! While we were there we went on a snorkeling adventure.

With us on the boat was a family of four; the children were young—about one and three. Over the course of the four-hour voyage I watched this couple as they tried to corral their two young children, who of course had no sense of the potential repercussions of falling off the boat in open water. The parents were like a tag team, alternating their watch on each child, managing temper tantrums, doing their best to come up with creative ways to engage their two toddlers. They were "in the weeds," as they say, and I found myself thinking, *Thank goodness I am no longer in that stage!* as I relaxed on the bow of the boat.

The thing is, when our kids are young we parents spend a lot of time simply trying to cope, trying to get through a stage, through a week, through a day. I recall our first family vacation, when my kids were one and three: trying to stuff them into snow suits and keep them warm; trying to unpack the car with kids wrapped around my ankles and crying to be picked up. I remember how hard it seemed then, and how I couldn't imagine the carefree days when the kids could actually help unload the car and have adult conversations with us. It seems like yesterday that they were that small, and soon, before I know it they may not even want to go on family vacations anymore, preferring to spend time with their friends instead of with us.

It is critical, both for our kids and for us, to find ways to create meaningful moments during the time we have together. Did you know there are only 940 Saturdays between a child's birth and her leaving for college? If your child is five years old, 260 of those Saturdays are already gone! And the older that kids get, the busier their Saturdays are with friends and activities. Depending on your child's age and school, activities, and your work schedule, there may be as little as one or two hours a day during the week for you to spend with them.

Instead of worrying about how much time we spend with our kids, one of the best ways we can help them become resilient, enjoy them as parents, and function well as a family is to focus on turning the time we do have into meaningful time and cultivating rich relationships with them. Not every day with your kids is going to be perfect. We are going to make mistakes, be irritated, want to pull out our hair, but a few meaningful moments can go a long way. These become the moments our kids remember, the ways they will define us as parents, and the keys to maintaining a healthy relationship as they get older. In fact, research suggests that a sense of connection is one of three components all people need to thrive and feel successful along with feeling competent and having a sense of control over their actions and behavior.

There are many aspects to cultivating relationships with kids that help them become more resilient to stress and adversity and also help us bond with them instead of just caring for them. Good relationships require putting down the phone, tearing our faces away from the computer—both of you!—and looking each other in the eye. Good relationships depend on good communication. They rest on how we talk to our kids, both when there's something wrong and when they've just scored the winning goal or won the national debate competition. It also means encouraging kids to cultivate relationships with other adults whom you trust and who care about them, whether that's a grandparent, an aunt, a favorite teacher, or the parent of your child's friend. Having a rich network of adult and peer relationships that involves healthy communication styles is one of the best ways we can help our kids develop empathy, an ability to feel what others feel in a given situation, not just feel sorry for them. Not only does empathy give kids a natural resiliency in the face of stress, but it is also the single best preventive strike against bullying.

We spend so much time these days trying to correct and deal with bullying after it has happened, when we could be doing so much more to prevent its development in the first place. By the time our children reach adulthood, they have seen two hundred thousand acts of violence demonstrated as a problem-solving technique. As a country, we spend a billion dollars a year on programs that help kids "unlearn" some of this propensity. Clearly the behaviors we are nurturing aren't matching up to our values.

Texting and the Internet may prove less violent than being beaten up at recess , but you don't need me to tell you that bullying is so much more easily done via electronic means than face-to-face. Part of the reason this is true rests with the parts of the brain we engage and develop in face-to-face communication and interaction.

It turns out that face time, especially in competition with screen time, is waning under the force of our modern lives. It also happens that face time has been evolutionarily critical to our development as thinking human beings. As we spend less face time with our kids—and as they get less time from their teachers as a result of increased class sizes, and from their peers and adults because they, the kids, are looking down at their phones instead of stopping to engage in conversation (and the peers and parents do the same)—the pathways in their brains are being altered. They are being rewired to be less empathic, less compassionate, and less able to connect in ways that nurture their resilience to adversity.

What's Happening in the Brain

Cognitively, we all have potential hardwired into our brains that is the result of generations of evolution as human beings. For example, we have evolved to have the capacity for speech and language development. Children can be taught to read and write and speak in any given language. But they do not naturally speak any one particular language; nor do they spontaneously develop language if they are not introduced to it by other humans. We know from a few striking examples in history that children who are raised in the absence of language, who are never spoken to nor hear words spoken aloud, do not develop language skills on their own. We also know that children who are spoken to very rarely while growing up have difficulty acquiring language and speech. So while the potential is there, latent in their brains, it takes the proper conditioning in the form of repeated and systematic cognitive experiences to have children learn to read and write. It's not enough to have the potential; they must be taught in order for this part of their brain to be activated as it was genetically programmed to.

I've borrowed the analogy of language acquisition from psychologist Bruce Perry, who uses it very effectively to explain the latent potential we all have in our brains to develop empathy, a keystone to building relationships and regulating our emotions. That latent potential, however, is not enough. We need the proper conditioning to develop and strengthen those neural pathways. You might remember from chapter 2 the evolution of human beings from living in larger, dense groups, with high ratios of adults to children, to modern times, when we are increasingly isolated in our homes, in our jobs, and in front of screens. That increasing isolation is akin to having language withheld from our environments and to not having language actively taught to us—with similar effects. Our decreased opportunities for interactions with other people, our decreased face time with other humans, is leading to a form of what is called "relational starvation." Without that sociological immersion, our latent potential for empathic connections with other people isn't being developed. We aren't developing the same skills related to empathy that we used to. This is problematic for all sorts of reasons, chief among them that empathy is our best natural defense against stress.

From an evolutionary standpoint, we are neurobiologically designed to feel safest when we belong to and are part of a group. In the brain, the stress response is lowered when we are around familiar people. Your heart beats more slowly and more regularly, and your breathing deepens and slows. Your digestive system is able to function properly because your body isn't on high alert. Even if we don't realize it is doing so, our brain is busy decoding and reflecting either calm and love or stress and tension as they are presented to us via the behavior of others. When we are around people who are calm, soothing, and happy, these emotions are naturally invoked in our brain, our mirror neurons firing in response to soothing tones of voice, to smiles and other pleasing facial expressions, and to slow, deliberate movements. When we aren't around familiar people (our "tribe"), we are more naturally stressed as our brain tries to determine if we are indeed safe in this strange group or in danger. Our stress response kicks in, making us physiologically, emotionally, and cognitively vulnerable to stress. Every face-to-face encounter we have throughout a given day presents an opportunity either for our stress response to fire or for the beneficial physiological effects of being part of a tribe to help keep us on an even keel.

How We're Starving Our Kids

In his keynote address to the Neurons to Neighborhoods Conference in Los Angeles, Perry illustrated what relational starvation looks like by following one child through an average day, detailing every physiological interaction he might have. A healthy child has a lot of "face time." He has rich interactions with his immediate family. He has a circle of friends and also a robust group of acquaintances. He gets positive feedback from his family and friends and even from the strangers he encounters throughout his day—a woman smiles at him on the bus, a little kid waves at him from a car window.

On the other end of the spectrum is a high-risk child who may experience many days when he has no face-to-face interactions at all. He wakes and eats breakfast by himself, and then finds his own way to school. On the bus no one sits with him or near him, and everyone avoids eye contact with him; he has been deemed the "weird" kid at school. No one sits with him at lunch, either, or says hi to him in the halls. He's largely ignored in class by both students and the teachers, *if* he behaves. If he doesn't get into trouble, in fact, he might get through the day without a single person talking to him. Even though getting in trouble doesn't seem like fun, you can see now why he might misbehave just to have a little contact with someone. You can also see how, predisposed to a stress response and chronic stress, this child would also set off unwanted behavior.

Now let's take that healthy child and alter his day a bit (in pretty common ways). He wakes up at the same time as his whole family, but his mom is yelling out orders and reminders to the kids and rushing to get herself ready for work. His dad is answering e-mails on his phone and scanning the headlines of the paper. The kid eats breakfast with his eyes glued to the television, and his sister, sitting next to him, does the same. The only time they talk is when she asks him to pass the milk. He walks to the bus listening to his iPod and texting his friends on his phone, then does this all the way to school once on the bus. At school he talks with his friends between classes and takes a brief break for lunch with his buddy, but after school he goes straight to football practice, where he does drills with his teammates and then heads home. Because it's late, he heats up his dinner and eats it standing in the kitchen while watching television. He goes to his room to do homework, mess around on the computer, and text his friends. This isn't a disadvantaged child, but he is a bit relationally starved. You can see how limited his real-time, present connections with people are.

Is Empathy on the Decline?

The result of our relationally starved children is a sharp decline in empathy among young people. One study examined the responses of fourteen thousand college students who had completed a questionnaire related to different types of empathy. The results showed that these students' average experience of "empathic concern," what we would call empathy, dropped by 48 percent between 1979 and 2009. The students' ability even to imagine someone else's point of view declined by 34 percent, with the steepest drop occurring between 2000 and 2009. Among the suspects for this steep decline were overuse and prevalence of media and personal technology, smaller family sizes wherein kids didn't have siblings to help teach them empathy, and increased academic pressures.

It's no accident that at the same time as we're seeing empathy on the decline, bullying behaviors seem to be on the rise. A study in *Educational Psychology* suggests that underdeveloped "affective empathy"—the ability to put oneself in someone else's shoes—occurs in high rates among bullies. A study of a group of 205 sixth-graders showed that bullies understood that their victims felt bad, but they were unable to internalize that pain to the point where it deterred them from causing the suffering in the first place.

The good news is that this is easier to turn around than you might think. While developing good relationships and fostering interconnectedness are the most powerful tools for promoting empathy, even the mere suggestion of social connection works, too. In a 2010 research experiment published in the journal *Psychological Science,* eighteen-month-old infants were shown photos of easily recognized household objects. For each photo, the background had one of four images: two dolls facing away from each other, one doll, two dolls facing each other, or building blocks. Infants who saw the photos that included the dolls facing each other were three times more likely than the others to help a peer or adult in need immediately following seeing the photos. Another research experiment had participants read words commonly associated with social connection—words such as *relationship* and *community*—before asking people how much they would volunteer for charity work. Participants were more willing to volunteer after reading connectedness words than they were after reading neutral words or words associated with either autonomy or competence, the other two of the three core components considered necessary for people to thrive. When participants of another study were asked to write about a close connection they had experienced personally, evoking that feeling of connection was enough to elicit a greater willingness to perform a variety of "prosocial" behaviors, such as helping a stranger or donating money to charity. In addition to promoting ideas of connectedness, mindfulness is a great tool (you will remember from the last chapters) for helping us develop empathy. Formal and informal mindfulness programs help strengthen the parts of our brains where empathic reasoning takes place.

The Building Blocks to Healthy, Successful, Responsible Kids

In 2011 the nonprofit Search Institute conducted an extensive study of American families with an eye toward identifying and building a framework of the positive experiences, relationships, opportunities, and qualities kids need in order to grow up healthy, caring, and responsible people. These "developmental assets," as Search calls them, are used extensively by educators, therapists, youth groups, and others who have a role in positively influencing and guiding children. I especially like them because they are grounded in research and focus on the same themes I have addressed in this book, those of building resiliency and preventing bad outcomes before they occur. In other words, helping our children thrive.

I encourage you to take a look at the developmental assets Search provides for each age group, beginning with preschoolers ages three to five on up to teens (www.searchinstitute.org). In the list that follows, the first twenty relate to external factors in a child's environment, such as good communication, being part of a community that values children and their input, and living in a safe, caring neighborhood. The second twenty detail internal factors that the child herself has control over, such as doing homework on time and having healthy self-esteem. You will notice that many of the factors Search found to decrease high-risk behavior and promote success rely on healthy relationships, interconnectedness, and empathic behaviors related to integrity and responsibility.

FORTY DEVELOPMENTAL ASSETS® FOR MIDDLE CHILDHOOD (AGES 8–12)

Support

1. **Family support**—Family life provides high levels of love and support.
2. **Positive family communication**—Parent(s) and child communicate positively. Child feels comfortable seeking advice and counsel from parent(s).

3. **Other adult relationships**—Child receives support from adults other than his parent(s).
4. **Caring neighborhood**—Child experiences caring neighbors.
5. **Caring school climate**—Relationships with teachers and peers provide a caring, encouraging environment.
6. **Parent involvement in schooling**—Parent(s) are actively involved in helping the child succeed in school.

Empowerment

7. **Community values youth**—Child feels valued and appreciated by adults in the community.
8. **Children as resources**—Child is included in decisions at home and in the community.
9. **Service to others**—Child has opportunities to help others in the community.
10. **Safety**—Child feels safe at home, at school, and in her neighborhood.

Boundaries and expectations

11. **Family boundaries**—Family has clear and consistent rules and consequences and monitors the child's whereabouts.
12. **School boundaries**—School provides clear rules and consequences.
13. **Neighborhood boundaries**—Neighbors take responsibility for monitoring the child's behavior.
14. **Adult role models**—Parent(s) and other adults in the child's family, as well as nonfamily adults, model positive,

responsible behavior. Child's closest friends model
positive, responsible behavior.

16. **High expectations**—Parent(s) and teachers expect the
child to do his best at school and in other activities.

Constructive use of time

17. **Creative activities**—Child participates in music, art,
drama, or creative writing two or more times per week.

18. **Child programs**—Child participates two or more times
per week in co-curricular school activities or structured
community programs for children..

19. **Religious community**—Child attends religious programs
or services one or more times per week.

20. **Time at home**—Child spends some time most days both
in high-quality interaction with parents and doing things
at home other than watching TV or playing video
games.

Commitment to learning

21. **Achievement motivation**—Child is motivated and strives
to do well in school.

22. **Learning engagement**—Child is responsive, attentive,
and actively engaged in learning at school and enjoys
participating in learning activities outside school.

23. **Homework**—Child usually hands in homework on time.

24. **Bonding to school**—Child cares about teachers and other
adults at school.

25. **Reading for pleasure**—Child enjoys and engages in
reading for fun most days of the week.

Positive values

26. **Caring**—Parent(s) tell the child it is important to help other people.
27. **Equality and social justice**—Parent(s) tell the child it is important to speak up for equal rights for all people.
28. **Integrity**—Parent(s) tell the child it is important to stand up for one's beliefs.
29. **Honesty**—Parent(s) tell the child it is important to tell the truth.
30. **Responsibility**—Parent(s) tell the child it is important to accept personal responsibility for behavior.
31. **Healthy lifestyle**—Parent(s) tell the child it is important to have good health habits and an understanding of healthy sexuality.

Social competencies

32. **Planning and decision making**—Child thinks about decisions and is usually happy with results of her decisions.
33. **Interpersonal competence**—Child cares about and is affected by other people's feelings, enjoys making friends, and, when frustrated or angry, tries to calm himself.
34. **Cultural competence**—Child knows and is comfortable with people of different racial, ethnic, and cultural backgrounds and with her own cultural identity.
35. **Resistance skills**—Child can stay away from people who are likely to get him in trouble and is able to say no to doing wrong or dangerous things.
36. **Peaceful conflict resolution**—Child seeks to resolve conflict nonviolently.

Positive identity

37. **Personal power**—Child feels she has some influence over things that happen in her life.
38. **Self-esteem**—Child likes and is proud to be the person he is.
39. **Sense of purpose**—Child sometimes thinks about what life means and whether there is a purpose to his life.
40. **Positive view of personal future**—Child is optimistic about her personal future.

The concept is simple, yet grounded in a cascade of research on risk and resiliency. Essentially, the more assets kids have, the less likely they are to engage in risky behaviors (do drugs, use alcohol, have sex, be violent) and the more likely they are to thrive (do well in school, demonstrate leadership qualities, eat well, etc.). While the ideal number of assets for kids is thirty or more, Search Institute research shows that, on average, young people count less than twenty of the assets, with boys faring slightly worse than girls. What is interesting in relation to this chapter is that so many of these assets can be directly influenced by positive relationships with adults.

The first time I learned about the assets, I was asked to picture an adult who had profoundly influenced my childhood. The person who came to mind was my elementary school physical education teacher, Mr. Cole. My earliest memory of school is of entering his gym for the first time. He had us all sit in a line at one end of the gym and then told us his expectations of us for class. I remember him saying in a very stern voice, "There is one word that you are *never* allowed to say in this gym!" He paused after that pronouncement. We were in rapt attention, our eyes as big as saucers with anticipation. "It is a four-letter word," he added. Our eyes grew wider.

What was he about to say? "That word is *can't*! You can say just about anything in here, but I never, ever want to hear you say, 'I can't.'" Mr. Cole knew a lot about motivation, specifically about instilling in kids something called a "growth mind-set," a topic we'll cover in more detail in the next chapter. People who exhibit a growth mind-set aren't afraid to rise to a challenge, there is nothing they believe they can't do, and they are resilient to challenge and change.

It wasn't just his ability to foster the growth mind-set that made Mr. Cole so special, but also his understanding of the primacy of connectedness. He would arrive at school early and open up the gym so that kids whose parents had to work early could drop in for some fun before the school day started. He also formed a running group called the Kilometer Club, which he supervised on his own time. When it was your birthday he would come barging into your classroom singing and dancing, and make a big show of your special day. He went out of his way to get to know his students, to listen, and to give advice. He was so much more than simply our PE teacher. When I looked at that list of assets with Mr. Cole in mind, I realized he had directly influenced nearly all of them. One teacher, one relationship, had a tremendous influence on my childhood and helped make me who I am today.

One of the things that really resonates with me about the Search Institute's developmental assets, in addition to the fact that they are grounded in solid research, is how they bring us back to our evolutionary core. They emphasize the importance of face-to-face relationships and the fact that it takes a village (or a clan) to raise healthy children. The basic guide isn't a magic bullet, but rather, a simple framework: Try to foster as many of the forty developmental assets in your kids as possible. In addition to the assets, here are a few more ideas for fostering connectedness in your family and increasing empathic responses in your kids.

A great way to connect your child's different "communities" at school and home is to participate regularly at your child's school. Not only is family participation in education *twice* as predictive of students' academic success as family socioeconomic status, but it also helps strengthen your understanding of your kid's school life and reflects your interest. And the more intensely parents are involved, the more beneficial the achievement effects.

Decades of research show that when parents are involved at school, students have:

* Higher grades, test scores, and graduation rates;
* Better school attendance;
* Increased motivation;
* Higher self-esteem;
* Lower rates of suspension;
* Decreased use of drugs and alcohol; and
* Fewer instances of violent behavior.

When parents come to school regularly, it reinforces the view in the child's mind that school and home are connected and that school is an integral part of the whole family's life. For me, it is also a great opportunity to get to know the kids in my child's class. I gain an understanding of personalities and group dynamics and can better participate in conversations with my child about school.

Solutions: Building Nurturing, Protective Relationships and Developing Empathy

One of the best ways to build healthy relationships with your child and increase his feelings of connectedness is through family

If you do not work full time, you might consider one or several of the following:

* Volunteer weekly in your child's classroom.
* Volunteer regularly in the library, front office, lunch room, or as a recess monitor.
* Offer to help in an area of personal interest—help the school institute a recycling program, volunteer to mentor the student council, or start a club.
* Help with fund-raising or special events.

If you do work full time, you might participate in this way:

* Schedule an afternoon off to chaperone a class field trip.
* Come in to the classroom to share your area of expertise. (If you are a doctor, speak to the kids about ways they can stay healthy, etc.)
* Offer to share the story of an event or holiday specific to your culture.
* Offer to prep materials at home for an upcoming classroom project. (Teachers have many projects that require material preparation. Prepping materials at home with your child will help engage her in the project and reinforce the message that education is important to you.)

rituals. Though we often think of rituals as being religion based, there are scores of fun rituals and traditions you can create—around holidays, yes, but also birthdays, or even Tuesdays! Here are a few of my favorites that we use in my family:

ALL AGES

- Include a bedtime ritual in your daily life and use it as source of connection. For younger kids this might be snuggling or reading stories, while for older kids it might include talking or listening to music together. In our house, Macy and I meditate together before bed.

- Create your own family night. Ours started when we first moved to Steamboat. I had no friends, I wasn't working, and I spent my days with a one-year-old and a three-year-old. By the time Friday rolled around I was dying to be out in the world, and usually ready for a margarita at the Mexican place down the street. So we made it a ritual to bundle the kids into the double stroller, grab the dog, and stroll into town. We had Mexican food, I got my margarita, and we all had a great time. On the stroll back we would often stop for a treat before going home. Recently my daughter declared "family night" the favorite of her holidays. It might have started with a need for adult talk and happy hour, but it turned into many "happy hours" for all of us.

- Once a year I go through all our photos from the past year and create a photo album book as my Christmas gift to my husband. It's a great way to control the chaos that is the jumble of photos from the year and a wonderful way to relive all the great memories, from trips to birthdays to hikes.

- Holiday rituals can be rich family time and a wonderful way to build relationships. The day after Thanksgiving, we all go over to Kenny's dad's house and have a huge brunch—bagels, lox, whitefish—you name it. Every Christmas, "Rudolph" brings my kids new pajamas and delivers them to the porch on Christmas Eve.

+ On the weekends we join a group of families in a pick-up game of soccer and a well-earned donut run. Anyone who is in town and interested shows up, both parents and kids, keeping it informal and low stress.

+ I don't schedule any activities or make plans on Mondays. I pick up the kids, and we head over to the library. We have hot chocolate, and the kids try to clear out as much of their week's homework as they can, freeing up the rest of the week for fun.

+ Use technology to your advantage. Skype is a great way for our kids to talk to their grandparents, who live far away.

+ My husband has a standing meeting that we take as an opportunity, the kids and I, to eat a special dinner in front of the TV and watch Macy's favorite, *American Idol*. She gets to jump around and sing and dance, and we enjoy the healthy stress of watching the competition.

+ Every Thursday, we walk or bike to school. It's so great to get out of the car and start talking!

+ Have your children create special rituals they enjoy with other adults. When we go on vacation to the shore, Kenny's dad chooses a different grandchild each morning to go with him to get the morning papers. When my dad visits, he takes my kids to an old-fashioned lunch counter in town for a special lunch and a shake.

+ On birthdays, we take turns giving our appreciation for the birthday boy or girl. This goes for parents and kids.

In addition to rituals, here are some more ideas for building relationships and connectivity with your kids:

Early Childhood (ages 0–5)

- Create something special that the two of you do each night. It can be talking about the best part of your day, singing a special song, or telling a funny story. These are the rituals kids remember years after you are tucking them into bed. This is a great one for elementary-age kids as well.

Elementary (ages 5–10)

- Take the extra time to walk or ride bikes to and from school or the bus stop instead of driving. This can create priceless moments that are easily sacrificed to the convenience of our cars. Take your time, listen to your kid, and look him in the eye. It is as good for you as it is for him!
- As the weather gets warmer, take advantage of the fresh air in the evenings and do a little stargazing. Have your kids ready for bed—pj's on, teeth brushed—then head outside with a blanket and spend ten minutes gazing at the sky.
- Eat dinner as a family—you knew this was coming. Make family dinners a priority, and use this time to engage and have fun, not fight over eating enough broccoli. Keep the kids happy and engaged, and they will eat.
- Become the student and let your child teach you a thing or two. We forget how much our kids learn every day. Take the time to listen mindfully after you ask them to teach you something they've learned. Start with the way they do addition—it's different from when we were kids!

Tweens (ages 10–13)

- A great idea for all age groups is cooking with your kids. (Be willing to sacrifice the cleanliness of the kitchen for some meaningful moments.) Dinner needs to be made, so why not turn the task into quality time spent together? Kids are also more likely to eat what they've made and be more adventurous in what they try.
- Play catch! With so many forms of entertainment, it seems the classic parent-child experience of playing catch has gone by the wayside. Playing catch is not just about learning to throw and catch; it is about the conversations that occur during the process.
- Get in touch with your own inner child and take them to see their favorite band in concert

Teens (ages 13–18)

While I've listed here some suggestions for strengthening the bond with your teen, one of the best ways to capture a teen's attention is to crank up the adrenaline factor. In the next chapter, I'll talk about how changes in a teen's brain actually make him crave risk, and joining your teen on more nail-biting adventures, whether it's careening on a zip line or learning to surf, is a great way to channel that need for "danger" into something less risky while strengthening your relationship with your teen by paying attention to his interests. See solutions at the end of the next chapter for more ideas.

- Divide and conquer. When you spend time one-on-one with a child, you can create conversations that don't occur when her younger sister or brother is vying for attention or listening in on what your teen might consider private information. Whether it is a trip to the store, making dinner together, or a enjoying special weekend away, spending time with just one of your children can be incredibly rewarding.

- Instead of making your teen responsible only for the garden chores (weeding, mowing the lawn), plant a garden with him. Choose seeds or seedlings together and do the weeding and watering as a team. Gardening is a great mindfulness activity and a fun way to "unplug" your teen. This is a great activity for all age groups if you vary the level of responsibility.
- Create a family football pool. Join a Fantasy Football league together—there are lots out there. The wager is irrelevant; it's about the weekly conversations that last the year round.
- Go to sporting events together to support your favorite team.
- If the kids are feeling too old for game night, why not up the ante and make it family poker night instead?
- If grandparents live close by, make an arrangement where your teen regularly goes over to help out her grandparents with chores or physical tasks they might not be able to do as well anymore. It inculcates in your teen a sense of service to others while building a stronger bond between generations. Take advantage of your teen's age and abilities and make him your hunting, fishing, or even foraging partner. Go into the mountains and pick berries or hunt for wild mushrooms. Or take your teen hunting or fishing. A friend takes his son salmon fishing in Alaska every year, just the two of them. But you don't need a guided trip or to fly anywhere to make it special.

ELEVEN

Cultivating Good Stress

Nearly every parent I know with more than one kid understands this phenomenon all too well. You have one child who's like a rubber floor mat; he can stand up to anything. You can wreck his routine, keep him out until midnight, throw him into play with a group of strangers, or feed him Thai street food for dinner, and he won't bat an eye. He volunteers to play new games and always seems ready for what's next. So much so that it doesn't seem possible he is even related to his sibling, who is less like rubber than silk, or maybe even paper.

This is the child who shrinks at the idea of doing a new activity without both a best friend by her side or you watching every moment from five steps away. This is the child who eats only white foods, or brown foods, but never orange foods, or nothing if any of the foods on the plate touch. This child is wrecked for two days if you tweak the bedtime routine by so much as ten minutes. This is the child who can't wear anything with pockets because it doesn't *feel* right.

Or you may have the child who is a mix of the two. Certain disturbances in the routine seem to roll right off his back, while other situations throw him into a complete tizzy. He is a great eater but a horrible sleeper. He is adventurous socially, but avoids all physical challenges.

My point is that some kids (and adults) are more resilient to the stress response than others.

There are lots of theories about why two kids in the same family with much of the same genetic makeup might turn out so different. Maybe it's the older child who seems sensitive while the younger is more robust. This is often attributed to birth order, a tacit suggestion that it was you who messed up your first one by walking on eggshells when she was born. Maybe one is a girl and one is a boy, or one is tall and the other petite. I've heard (and even suggested) some of these same theories, because I have two kids, one a girl and one a boy, born two years apart from each other, who are not quite as different as the examples I've just given—but let's just say I have an understanding of kids with different capacities.

The good news, and the lesson I hope you've learned by now, is that our brains are malleable. If we change our behavior, we also change our brains—meaning there is a lot we can do to increase resiliency to stress for those kids who tend to have a narrow window of tolerance. We can help them develop a growth-oriented mind-set, provide them with strategies for dealing with negative thoughts, and present opportunities to overcome obstacles in a healthy way, which together can make a huge difference. Those neural pathways that when presented with a challenge used to say, "I can't," will subtly shift to something more like "Maybe I can."

However, it's not just kids who exhibit this range in their window of tolerance to the unfamiliar or to stress. (We talked a bit about helicopter parents, who tend to have a narrow tolerance for stress, in chapter 5, and we'll talk more about them in this chapter.) How many couples do you know who are made up of one person who attends every party happily and one who hovers, pained, near the door? Or perhaps you have one friend who lives to travel on the fly, while another has a printed checklist just for going out of town for the weekend?

You may not be surprised to learn that there is a neurobiological component to these differences. People really are wired differently, with some folks exhibiting brains structurally more open and resilient to change and stress. For others, every little stressor—even an annoying sound or an unexpected wait—is a new opportunity to become completely derailed. During adolescence, our brains go through special changes that affect our capacity for stress and promote an urge to seek out risk. Let's take a closer look at the differences between narrow and wide windows of tolerance on a cognitive level before we get to different ways we can work to widen those windows and increase resiliency to stress, building on all the good changes we're already making with increased empathy and mindfulness.

What's Happening in the Brain

You may remember from earlier chapters a neurotransmitter called serotonin, which is associated with elevated mood and a sense of calm. Serotonin is produced in the body using the amino acid tryptophan, famous as the "Thanksgiving nap" chemical because high levels of tryptophan are found in turkey, but also in chocolate, dairy, and other foods we associate with comfort and pleasure, and which we often eat to get a mood "boost." We also release serotonin into our bodies when we exercise, a reason exercise is a powerful way to combat depression.

Many people are familiar with serotonin because of a class of medications called SSRIs, or selective serotonin reuptake inhibitors, a type of antidepressant that treats anxiety and depression by blocking the reabsorption of serotonin, leaving more of it available to the brain. While chronic stress or pain can lower serotonin levels, some people naturally have lower levels of serotonin available to them, or their serotonin is reabsorbed more quickly, leaving less time for that feeling of calm and pleasure to override feelings of anxiety or depression. In 2004, a Duke University Medical Center research study found that people with low levels of serotonin were more likely to suffer from heart disease compared to people with average or high serotonin levels, likely due to their compromised ability to handle stress.

There are other differences in the brain that affect someone's ability to handle stress. Some people have more active, denser, or larger amygdalae than others, giving them a propensity toward an increased stress response. There can be differences in the prefrontal cortex as well that make some people more able than others to access their "thinking brains." These are all neurological differences that might affect our children, making some seem more fragile and less able to handle stress than others.

Parents of teenagers often face an issue on the other end of the spectrum. Instead of having kids who can't handle the "risk" of going to sleepaway camp or taking a class in something they don't excel in, teenagers can shift into a mode where they seem to seek out risk, whether it's in the form of driving too fast, drinking and taking drugs, or hanging out with the "wrong" crowd. New research has revealed differences in adolescent brains that also explain this behavior.

The Adolescent Brain

When he was in eighth grade my nephew's class took a trip to an amusement park in Portland. Sounds like every kid's dream school day, doesn't it? Well, he didn't want to go. He was terrified—not of a roller coaster of death or the Hammerhead that spins you in nauseating circles sixty feet off the ground, the centrifugal force making your innards crawl up your throat. No, his nemesis was a ride called the Frog Hopper. Go ahead, look up some videos on YouTube. You'll see delighted, screaming three- and four-year-olds safely strapped into padded seats as they are raised a few feet vertically in the air and then dropped toward the ground in short bursts. That's it. You move on only one axis, and not even very quickly. At the max, you're probably fifteen feet off the ground, and your feet are always ready to "break" your fall. It's a ride a typical three-year-old would go on again and again, but not my thirteen-year-old nephew.

Fast-forward to just over a year later. The same nephew is camping with a group between his freshman and sophomore years. Imagine my shock to watch recorded video of this formerly cautious boy taking a giant leap and flinging himself off a cliff to plunge into the water fifty feet below. Just watching the video made my heart stop, but there he was, clearly delighted. He was addicted to the danger, to the sheer thrill of it. Clearly, in the intervening year, some biological changes had happened in him that went beyond the two inches he had grown.

Emerging research is now better able to explain my nephew's leap from fear of the Frog Hopper to cliff diving mania. Understanding the neurobiological shift that occurs in adolescents is an important key to safely channeling and encouraging thrill-seeking behaviors.

I adore my two teenaged nephews; they are great kids. However, I must admit I'm amazed at the different set of pressures and nuances my sister and brother-in-law deal with as parents of teens. Their struggles are quite logical, though, in light of some fascinating new research that takes the conventional wisdom about adolescent behavior and tweaks it in a really interesting, and somewhat encouraging, way.

If you are the parent of a teen, you probably don't need me to tell you that teenagers can make somewhat irrational decisions. They can be impulsive, take wild risks, and sometimes jump first (literally) without thinking through the possible consequences of their actions. These actions range from the benign (texting with a girlfriend all night before a big test) to the downright dangerous (sneaking out to meet a stranger they've met online). Beginning in the 1990s, research on the brain explained this type of behavior as the result of an extended cerebral childhood. Children's brains don't reach maturity until they are in their twenties, the research suggested. They seem to make crazy choices because they just don't have the capacity to make good ones. Their bodies, we were told, are "older" than their brains.

We still recognize that during the teen years and into early adulthood important changes occur in the brain that work to make our thinking more sophisticated and our decision-making processes faster and more efficient. This happens due to changes to two different chemical junctures in the brain: long nerve fibers called axons and branchlike extensions called dendrites. As adolescents mature, the axons and dendrites become more insulated with a substance called myelin, which insulates the nerve fibers, boosting our "connection speed" in the process. While this is happening, we also become literally set in our ways. Synapses that get little use are passed over in favor of the strengthening of oft-used pathways. Maturing brains also develop better methods for integrating memory and experience into the decision-making process, something teens could be said to be sorely in need of: *When I do* x *the consequence is usually* y. *When* y *is undesirable, let's try* z *instead.*

While teenagers and young adults awkwardly learned to use their newly maturing brain, and make mistakes while doing so, conventional wisdom offered us all, researchers and parents, what psychologist David Dobbs has called "an alluringly pithy explanation for why teens may do stupid things," in the form of a conclusion that infantilized maturing teenagers and didn't offer parents much hope, besides waiting out the predestined time period during which adolescents act like idiots.

Yet newly emerging research has challenged this thinking, and could change the paradigm of the risk-seeking teenager and how we approach our teens as mindful parents. When they looked at evolutionary theory (just as we did with empathy), researchers have found that teens aren't crazy. They are, in fact, propelled physiologically into being less risk averse than adults. While adolescent brains may not possess the finely honed decision-making skills of an adult brain, there appears to be a good reason teens crave risk. In fact, this new research "casts the teen less as a rough draft than as an exquisitely sensitive, highly adaptive creature wired almost perfectly for the job of moving from the safety of the home into the complicated world outside."

Teens aren't illogically impulsive, but instead value novelty and risk more highly than do adults. They may very deliberately choose to engage in what we consider high-risk activity and seek new experiences and thrills as part of a biological drive. As humans evolved, adolescence was the time when we started to take on more dangerous roles in the tribe. It was the teens who had the strength to fight off enemies, and the speed and dexterity to hunt for food. Without this bolder, risk-taking adventure, adolescents would never have left the nest and gone out on their own. The behavioral shift was essential to our survival as a species. Without teens' increased tolerance for risk and their pull toward adventure, we may very well not have survived.

Kathryn Bowers and Dr. Barbara Natterson-Horowitz found that the same is true in the animal kingdom. Looking at shared animal and human biological traits, they noted adolescent male otters regularly venturing into shark-infested waters that other otters avoided completely, and observed immature Thomson's gazelles strolling brazenly up to predators such as cheetahs or lions. They may be tempting fate, but they are also learning how to operate in the world on their own. This has led to the idea that increased adolescent impulsivity is not pathological, but is instead correlated with later social success in both animals and humans. Knowing not only the how but also the why allows us to better care for our teenagers and work with the brains they have, providing opportunities for "safe" risk taking and adventure that satisfy their biological urge for daring while keeping them alive.

Expanding Our Tolerance for Stress

So now we have two defined issues to deal with. One takes the form of widening the window of resiliency for kids who seem more prone to the stress response. The other lies in channeling a propensity for thrill-seeking behavior into what I call "safe risk," or activities that feel risky on a cognitive level but don't truly put the child in danger the way other high-risk activities (sex, drinking, and drugging) do.

One of the best ways I know to start off right in dealing with both situations rests in how we communicate with our kids, how we encourage them, and how we deliver praise. This is encompassed by promoting what I alluded to in the last chapter as a growth mind-set. In plain terms, a growth mind-set fosters independence and resiliency and decreases the devastating effects of perfectionism and a child's tendency to accept only what is familiar or known.

Fixed-vs.-Growth Mind-set

There has been a great deal of research around what psychologists call the fixed-vs.-growth mind-set, including some important research done by Carol Dweck at Stanford University. Dweck's research aims to find the underlying reasons for disproportionate success, or why, given equal talent, some people succeed while others don't. Part of the answer seems to lie in whether people, including kids, believe they are capable of achieving anything if they just set their minds to it (growth) or if they believe they were born with a set of skills and talents over which they have little control (fixed). It may seem simplistic to resort to the "you can do anything!" speech, especially with kids, but I invite you to listen to the messages we give our children on a daily basis:

> "You got one hundred percent on your spelling test!
>   You are so smart!"
> "Your team won! Let's go get ice cream!"
> "You are so talented. You played that piano piece perfectly!"

The SATs might be the only area where we don't expect our children to do or score *perfectly,* though the higher the score, the more praise the child is going to receive. Though it may seem from the description just given that anyone would prefer to have a growth mind-set, praising our children so much and so often, and for results rather than effort, can have an insidious effect. The result of praising your child only for winning the game, not for practicing hard leading up to the big day, or only for acing the test rather than for setting aside time to study diligently in the week leading up to the test, is that you highlight only the result. Dweck's research consistently demonstrates that this outcome-oriented praise has more negative consequences for students' achievement and motivation than praise for effort, or what I call process-oriented praise ("You must have worked really hard").

Let me give you another example. In a study of fifth-graders performing academic tasks, one group was given outcome-oriented praise. While they performed the task, they were told things such as "Wow! You must be really smart!" The other group was given process-oriented praise, told instead, "You are working really hard." The task got increasingly more difficult, and after failure, the group that was given outcome-oriented praise displayed less task persistence (they gave up sooner), less task enjoyment, more low-ability attributions (they felt bad about themselves when they didn't get it correct), and worse task performance. The students given process-oriented praise were more persistent, didn't beat themselves up if they made a mistake, and ultimately performed better. These findings have important implications for how achievement is best encouraged.

In real terms, what this looks like is that since your daughter is really good at soccer but only so-so at baseball, she won't turn out for the baseball team. If getting As is critical, your son might not try his hand at physics or another subject that he doesn't grasp outright. Also, anything less than perfect becomes equivalent to failure because everyone wants to be perceived as successful or smart. In order for fixed-mind-set people to be perceived as successful or smart, they need to demonstrate they "have it," which is the equivalent of winning the game or acing the test. So they avoid challenges and obstacles and give up quickly on things they don't have a natural aptitude for or that don't come easily. Dweck's work also shows that feedback given fixed-mind-set people is internalized as criticism, not of the effort but of the person. A fixed mind-set also reduces tendencies toward empathy, because the success of people around the fixed-mind-set individual is seen only in terms of competition and is considered a threat to his success. The effects can be devastating.

Like me, my daughter is very outcome oriented. She always has been. She loves to dance and she dances constantly. Every morning, afternoon, and evening she has the music on and is dancing around our house. One day she said to my husband and me, "Mom, you are an okay dancer, and Dad is a horrible dancer. How do you think I got to be so good?" My husband (rather congenially) said, "Macy, you work really hard at your dancing, you practice constantly, every day. It makes sense that you are so good, because you work so hard."

This statement really seemed to blow her away. In her outcome-oriented mind she was simply born a good dancer. Slowly, with a lot of effort on our part, she is starting to understand the process and the value of hard work. This has taken a lot of deliberate determination on our part as parents, with our being very intentional about how we praise. But it is working.

If you have an outcome-oriented kid, here are some ideas for how best to encourage the growth mind-set through

Examples of Process-Oriented Praise

Wow, you really worked hard out there!"
"All that time you spent practicing your spelling words sure
    paid off when you took the test."
"You guys must have worked hard in your practice, because it
    really showed in that game."
"I know you can do it if you put your mind to it!"
"You must be proud of all the work you put into that assignment!"

process-oriented praise. The key is to attribute success to things
such as effort, commitment, resourcefulness, hard work, and practice. My advice is to pick one or two statements that resonate with
you and use them to replace your usual outcome-oriented praise.
It takes effort, but it will get easier with time. It's also one of the
most important shifts we can make in our parenting. If our kids
believe that their dedication and effort matter, it can lead to a long
life of success stories and, more important, a lot of happiness!

Why a Growth Mind-set is Even More Imperative for Girls

One of the most critical reasons that encouraging a growth mind-
set with process-oriented praise is so important is that outcome-
oriented kids can fall into the trap of perfectionism—not willing
to do anything they don't excel in and beating themselves up for
even the smallest "failure." Because of societal pressures, this is
doubly true for girls. In his book *The Triple Bind,* psychologist

Stephen Hinshaw details how girls in modern society are hit doubly hard by these pressures, expected to be both perfectly traditional in what are considered female ways (attractive, cute, caring, pleasing, compassionate) while possessing traits in the male realm (competitive, strong, successful, assertive, and driven). These expectations are unrealistic, of course, but that is not the message we're sending our girls. The result is that they feel caught between being top in their class and balancing how others feel about their success, or being a strong athlete but not being feminine enough. A fixed mind-set says that anything less than perfect is failure. Hinshaw cites increased rates of suicide, violence, eating disorders, and depression among girls due to what he calls "the triple bind." In order to make girls resilient to these expectations of perfection and help them thrive, Hinshaw cites, among other solutions, quality relationships with adults and being part of a community as ways to help bolster girls' compassion toward themselves and others and give them increased self-esteem.

Conversely, a growth mind-set follows what we've learned about the neuroplasticity of our brains. We can grow, change, learn, and adapt depending on the behaviors we nurture. Growth mind-set people know that our brains are like muscles—when we flex them and use them, certain areas get denser and stronger and certain pathways are strengthened. In a growth mind-set, success is not the end goal; learning and practice are goals in and of themselves. You can see how this shift changes the pressure on a child and the emphasis on the desired behavior. Kids who are praised and encouraged to try new things, to make mistakes, to work hard at improvement, to approach problems creatively, and to work cooperatively have this growth mind-set reinforced.

With the growth mind-set, challenges become opportunities for learning, as opposed to threats to the individual's success and self-esteem. Growth mind-set people aren't as easily discouraged, have more tenacity, and are willing to work in teams or groups to achieve desired outcomes. Similarly, feedback is taken not as personal criticism but more at face value, and becomes a tool for learning. No, this doesn't mean a student will love every comment scrawled on his paper by his English teacher, but it could mean he is able to read the comments and use the information to avoid making the same mistake in the future, instead of having the feedback obscured by a personal sense of failure that there were any red marks on the paper at all. Growth mind-set people are able to process that information as being about how they, say, cited from sources for a term paper incorrectly or used their adverbs improperly, rather than see the comments as about them as people.

Encouraging a Growth Mind-set

The good news is that we all have the potential to be growth mind-set people, given the proper environment and reinforcements. The information we give our kids, and reinforce through communication such as praise, has a profound effect and can help budge even the most ardent fixed mind-set kids. A study by Carol Dweck and Lisa Sorich Blackwell put a group of seventh-graders with weak academic records into study skills classes. Half learned about memory while the other half learned about how our brains become strengthened through exercise and practice and about the fundamentals of a growth mind-set. While students in the memory class showed no improvement, those who were taught growth mind-set skills became more motivated and showed improvement in math skills.

Here's another, nonacademic example. Recently I gave a new talk entitled "Mindful Golf." While preparing it, I was once again reminded of how vital the mental part of athletics, and using a growth mind-set, is to achieving success. I think most people would agree that there is a physical, technical, and mental aspect to all sports, yet we all tend to spend 99 percent of our energy and money on the physical and technical aspects while secretly hoping that the mental aspects will simply fall into place.

The great athletes, the really great ones, the ones who become iconic figures, have a mental edge over their opponents. Think Michael Jordan, Tiger Woods (before the turmoil), Missy Franklin. Interviews with these sports stars reveal a focus on mental preparation and mental control. With that in mind, I began thinking about how little we talk to our kids about the mental side of sports: how to prepare, how to start a game, how to handle adversity when the game gets away from us.

Your child may be an amazing soccer player, faster and more skilled than her teammates, but if she loses all control when a goal is scored against her team, how successful can she ultimately be? With this in mind, here are a few more thoughts for nurturing a growth mind-set in your child. While these apply to sports, you can easily extrapolate and apply the same techniques to piano, math, cooking, or painting.

PROCESS-ORIENTED GOALS PHRASED
AS SELF-TALK

Help your child pick a process-oriented goal. Most of us tend to think in outcome-oriented ways. Your child may play incredibly well and still lose to his competitor who scores better. When we judge ourselves by parameters that are influenced by events out of our control, we set ourselves up to damage our confidence, which by nature is fragile and delicate.

We can't control what other players or teams do or their levels of skill. Great competitors focus on variables that *are* within their power to influence. They focus on the process, and winning becomes a pleasant bonus. Try to identify one process-oriented goal before each game or event:

I'm going to make ten great passes this half.

I'm going to attack fifty out of fifty balls.

I'm going to keep my glove down on ground balls.

I'm going to step out of the batter's box and take two
    deep breaths between each pitch.

I'm going to visualize every golf shot I take.

I'm going to follow through on all my tennis shots.

I'm going to scoop through, rather than rake, every ground
    ball at lacrosse practice.

Just as important, the next time you are playing catch, or passing the ball back and forth, or riding home from a practice or game with your child, ask him, "What was the hardest part of today's practice or game?" Then move the conversation to see what your child realized about the challenge of this situation, and what he can do in the future when this situation arises. It's a much different conversation from just saying, "You did great today!"—actually, it invites a conversation rather than being just a statement, and it reinforces a consistent problem-solving growth mind-set.

Another important component of this type of communication is to watch your nonverbals, or the cues you give your child in communicating with your body. The tilt of your head, the softness of your face, whether you are smiling or frowning—all demonstrate your real intent and feelings clearly. Make sure your nonverbal cues match the words you are saying to your child, thereby strengthening the positive communication and the positive emotions you hope to convey.

Breathing Life into the Power of Positive Thinking

You might have noticed that part of a growth mind-set is adjusting how we talk to ourselves and how we teach our kids to talk to themselves. As we learned in our discussion of mindfulness and empathy, we are often our own worst enemies, filling our heads with judgment, *can'ts* and *shoulds*. For younger kids, it can be difficult to explain in concrete terms the power of being kind to ourselves. A suggestion from Dr. Stephen Briers, author of *How Your Child Thinks,* harnesses the power of a young child's imagination to provide a fun way to combat negative self-talk.

Explain to your child that we all have voices inside us that say mean things or cause us to be afraid or worried. Those voices are not telling the truth; they are telling lies, and those lies are destined to hurt us. They say things like "You are terrible at math" or "Your hair looks awful" or "You or going to make a fool out of yourself if you try that!" Ask your child to imagine a creature, animal, or invented person who might be saying these things to her. Then have her draw a picture of the "villain" she has envisioned. Some kids might draw angry gods or witches or goblins. Some might draw bolts of lightning or scary animals. Ask your child to explain her drawing, using questions such as "How does your villain use his powers to make you feel bad?" or "Where

does your villain live when she's not saying mean things to you"?
Also, have your child name her villain to provide a shorthand for
talking about the villain whenever negative talk arises. Continue
the exercise with a concrete plan on how to banish the villain to
another world or fight against the villain's destructive weapons.
For example, if your child is afraid to go into class on the first day
of kindergarten, Zamora the Witch might be whispering to her
that she won't make any friends, that the teacher won't like her,
or that she won't be as smart as the other kids. If you are able to
talk about the lies Zamora is spreading, then you can reframe the
fears as untruths that must be battled, appealing to your child's
sense of fairness. Encourage her to go into school and show
Zamora how wrong she is by saying a bright hello to the teacher,
or by asking a classmate's name and then introducing herself.

Visualization works with everyone, of course. You might find
it helpful to picture the devil on your shoulder. Teens could liken
their inner destructive force to a video game character, a type of
music, or even an Internet virus corrupting the good "data"
stored in their brains.

Another common way of combatting negative thoughts, once
your mind is spinning out of control, is to reframe the horrific
scenario, asking yourself, *Is what I'm thinking true?* And then, *How
do I know it's true?* If your teen is agonizing over a friend being
mad at her, have her answer the next logical questions:

Is it true your friend is mad at you?

Yes!

How do you know this to be true?

She texted her friend an hour ago, and her friend didn't text
her back.

Well, her friend could be at an appointment, she could be doing homework, or maybe her phone battery ran out of juice.

Also, your teen didn't do anything she can remember that would have caused a rift.

Going through the exercise can demonstrate how our minds are primed to jump to the worst conclusion, even if we have to make great imaginative leaps to get there.

Creating Opportunities for Healthy Risk

Now that we've covered different ways to talk to kids to make them more resilient to stressful situations, you might be surprised by my next piece of advice. Intentionally place your children in "stressful" situations (i.e., give them opportunities to take risks, to encounter adventure, and to fail). In addition to fostering a growth mind-set and using the techniques just outlined to help less resilient kids cope with stress, encouraging kids to engage in an intentional form of healthy risk is good parenting.

Okay, I get it. Despite our discussion in chapter 5 of the effects of overparenting, I recognize you may still need some convincing. Sure, you might be saying, I see the reasoning behind praising hard work over outcomes. But why on earth would I want to let my eight-year-old whittle with a pocketknife?

First of all, by creating opportunities for kids to engage in adventure, you help those kids with a narrow window of stress tolerance widen that window bit by bit. Our brains remember the good stress of adventure, and they also take note when adventure results in a positive outcome. The roller coaster stops, and we get off. The zip line delivers us to a stable platform. We finish our mountain bike ride with no major wipeouts. Every time our adventures end well, our brain associates this good stress with a positive outcome. And even when their adventures don't go perfectly, when they wipe out on their bikes or while trying to ski down the black run, kids realize that though they have failed, they are still okay. They learn from this experience and know what to do differently the next time around.

This is why fostering healthy risk in kids who are more prone to a stress response can gradually work to widen their window of comfort in a safe and predictable way. We can't and shouldn't raise our kids in a bubble or protect them from every kind of stress, even if we understand that, biologically, they may be wired a bit differently. It's important for them to think of themselves (and for us as parents to retrain ourselves to think of them) as needing a little more warm-up or compassion leading to a new experience, but also as ultimately available and open to all sorts of opportunities.

By promoting healthy risk and adventure from the time they are young, we help our adolescents arrive at their teenage years with plenty of practice in making good decisions around challenges and new areas of interest or focus, and allow them to have lots of experience engaging in healthy risk under their belts. They are thus less likely than a sheltered or small-window teen to test their boundaries and limits just for the experience of doing so—please note I didn't say they won't test your boundaries at all!—or to turn automatically to unhealthy behaviors to generate a sense of thrill. Once they're teens, healthy risk provides real options for thrill-seeking that satisfy that biological urge for danger in appropriate ways that can also be really fun for the whole family!

The key to applying the healthy adventure suggestions listed here is to tailor them to your child's age and window of comfort. For example, if you're teaching a narrow-window five-year-old kid to ride a bike, you might run alongside him more or keep the training wheels on longer than for other kids, but it doesn't mean you should let him give up. Your twelve-year-old might be over-whelmed by the thought of competitive sports, but you can strengthen her resilience to stress and build her self-confidence through activities such as rock climbing and mountain biking. Remember, our brains react to events based on previous experiences, thus creating patterns of response. As kids are presented with a challenge such as a short backpacking trip or a more difficult bike ride or hike, their brains develop a pattern that allows them to handle adversity with the knowledge that they are capable of accomplishment. If you're a narrow-window parent, remember that it works the same way for you!

Solutions: Cultivating Good Stress

Early Childhood (ages 0–5)

- Take your young ones car camping. They get to experience the beauty of nature with many of the comforts of home, from cots to stuffed animals.
- Instead of driving your kids to school or day care, or even when you go on errands, walk or take the bus instead. Point out the different types of people and buildings you see.
- Even with really young ones you can put them in a backpack or in a designated child's seat and take a short hike or bike ride
- Teach your child to swim or have her learn in a class. Swimming builds independence and is a life-saving skill on its own.
- Around the age of three and up, kids are capable of learning to ice-skate and ski. They even have the advantage in being closer to the ground, with a lower center of gravity!

Elementary (ages 5–10)

- Give them horseback-riding lessons.
- Have your child take the family dog for a regular walk around the neighborhood.
- Teach your child how to ride a bike.
- Have the whole family go backpacking or mountain biking.
- Go on berry-picking trips in the woods.
- Take family ski trips.
- Let your child learn to ride a skateboard.
- Take the whole family to a water park or amusement park.
- Go tubing down a river in the summer.
- Take your older child hunting or fishing.
- Teach your child how to use a pocketknife responsibly and then whittle or use the knife when camping or hiking.
- Go swimming in the ocean or bodysurfing.
- Have your child make a birthday cake or cupcakes (with limited help from you) for someone.

Tweens (ages 10–13)

For tweens (this goes for teens as well), there is a host of outdoor activities that are tailor-made for young, resilient bodies just beginning to crave a jolt of adrenaline. Many, however, also require focus and can even extend to a form of mindfulness.

- Take your tween rock climbing or bouldering or sign her up for climbing classes or events.
- Allow your tween to go (gulp) cliff jumping, and maybe even try it yourself!

- Take your tween mountain biking.
- Strap your tween to a zip line, whether it's in a park or a rain forest.
- Take your tween parasailing.
- Have your tween learn to snowboard.
- Take your tween traveling abroad or to a country where they speak a different language, or enable him to go with a group or on a class trip.
- Give your tween the opportunity to learn to surf or boogie-board.
- Encourage (or allow) your tween to ride the subway or bus to a friend's house alone.
- Send your child to sleepaway camp. Not only will she receive a technology cleanse and enjoy the great outdoors, but it will build independence and resiliency.
- Have your child participate in a National Outdoor Leadership School (NOLS) trip or other group adventure—he might bike across the country or hike an interstate trail.
- Have her join a speech and debate club.
- Encourage your tween to try out for a sport he has never played.

Teens (ages 13–18)

- Encourage your kid to perform at a spoken-word or open-mic night, audition for a part in a play, or have her band perform in public.
- Instead of going out to dinner on a date, encourage your teen to cook dinner at your home for his date instead. This creates a great kind of healthy stress, especially for boys cooking to impress girls.

- Have your child write a regular blog or articles for the school paper or contribute to a zine or magazine. Putting your written work out there can feel very risky (trust me!).
- Encourage your child to develop skills or try something new while also helping others. Your teen might help build a house for Habitat for Humanity or do work with TeenCore.
- Encourage your teen to run for student council or participate with the local city government on a student board or advisory group.

Extensive, notated references are online at www.mindfullifetoday.com.

ACKNOWLEDGMENTS

I often refer to the saying, "It takes a village to raise a child." The same certainly can be said about the writing of a book. I never would have been able to write this book without the support of so many wonderful people.

I can't say enough about the amazing Leslie Miller. Lam, you made the writing part of this book the easiest part! Your wisdom, brilliance, sense of humor, and friendship were invaluable in this process. This book would not be the same without you! Thank you to my literary agent, Stephanie Kip Rostan, and my editor, Nichole Argyres, you both "got me" from the get-go and guided this book wonderfully. Thank you to my brilliant cousin Liz Race Terborgh for her insight into the chemistry of the brain.

The beliefs and philosophies rooted in this book are the product of so many inspiring and amazing people.

Sylvie Piquet, if anyone was born to be mindful it was you. I feel so grateful to have you in my life. Your brilliance, aptitude for working with children, random humming of tunes, and smile are a gift to us all. Thank you for all that you have meant to my work, my family, my life.

Thank you to the hundreds of teachers, counselors, parents, and caring community members around the world who have embraced Mindful Life and work to share our tools and strategies with children. Your passion for your work is an amazing gift to all of our children and a constant source of inspiration.

I am grateful to all of those who have come before me in the mindfulness movement. Jon Kabat-Zinn, Richard Davidson, Susan Kaiser Greenland, Rick Hanson, Congressman Tim Ryan, Christine Carter, Gina Biegel, and so many more, your work has motivated and inspired me. Thank you for all that you do to share mindfulness.

Thank you to everyone in the incredible Steamboat Springs community. Each day I am grateful for the opportunity to raise my family in this warm, thoughtful, friendly, fun, and supportive place.

Thank you to Bill and Karen Cole for being those teachers who change lives, you profoundly influenced who I am today, and thank you for all of the children's lives you touched throughout your amazing careers.

I am so grateful for the incredible friendships that instilled my belief in the power of relationships. Thank you to those from Denver to Cincinnati to San Fran who helped me learn the precious value of time to just hang out!

I am grateful to have two fantastic parents, Geoff and Carol, who have supported me, guided me, and been amazing role models as I strive to be the best parent and person I can be. Thank you to my incredible sisters, Lisa and Kim, who keep me laughing until I start to cry and whose work with children and families is a constant source of inspiration. A special thank-you to Lisa for all of your contributions to this book. Thank you to Kit, Kael, and Keaty, I love you all and am so fortunate to have you as part of my village. I am so grateful for all of "the Reisman" side of my family. I have learned so much from you all, including—it is okay to cry out of happiness, and to travel all the way across the country just to give someone a hug! I am so lucky to have you all in my life.

Macy and Charlie, you have given up a lot for me to be able to write this book. I treasure every day that I get to see your smiling faces. Thanks for understanding when I have to travel for work, thanks for the cards and pictures you make for me while I'm gone, and thanks for leaping into my arms with huge hugs and kisses every time I return.

Kenny, where to begin . . . thank you for the countless reads, edits, and opinions that have influenced this book. Thank you for always being the one to do the tasks that no one else wants to do. Thank you for your enduring faith in Mindful Life and your desire to dedicate your life to work that will make a difference for others. You are truly selfless in your commitment to support your community, your family, and all families. This book would never have been possible without you. I love you.

INDEX

ABOUT THE AUTHOR

Corey Kopischke

Kristen Race, Ph.D., is an expert in child, family, and school psychology and the founder of Mindful Life. Dr. Race speaks regularly at national conferences and for many community groups. Her print articles have appeared in *Kiwi* magazine, *Denver Life,* and *Colorado Business Magazine,* among others, and she has appeared on *CBS This Morning* and *Everyday Colorado* as a parenting expert. She lives in Steamboat Springs, Colorado, with her family.